Almost Free Gold!

How to Earn a Quick $1000 Finding Gold, Silver and Platinum Where You Live

Eric Michael

Copyright, Legal Notice and Disclaimer:

This publication is protected under the US Copyright Act of 1976 and all other applicable international, federal, state and local laws, and all rights are reserved, including resale rights: you are not allowed to give or sell this Guide to anyone else.

Please note that much of this publication is based on personal experience and anecdotal evidence. Although the author and publisher have made every reasonable attempt to achieve complete accuracy of the content in this document, they assume no responsibility for errors or omissions. Also, you should use this information as you see fit, and at your own risk. Your particular situation may not be exactly suited to the examples illustrated here; in fact, it's likely that they won't be the same, and you should adjust your use of the information and recommendations accordingly.

Any trademarks, service marks, product names or named features are assumed to be the property of their respective owners, and are used only for reference. There is no implied endorsement if we use one of these terms.

Finally, use your head. Nothing in this Guide is intended to replace common sense, legal, medical or other professional advice, and is meant to inform and entertain the reader. There is no guarantee of financial success.

Copyright © 2014 Eric Michael. All rights reserved worldwide

Readers' Praise for Almost Free Money

5.0 out of 5 stars

The author is a money-making machine

By **Bill Nelson**

This review is from: Almost Free Money: How to Make Extra Money on Free Items That You Can Find Anywhere, Including Garage Sales, Thrift Shops, Scrap Metal and Finding Gold (Kindle Edition)

"This guy is like a money-making machine. Almost Free Money: How to Make Significant Money on Free Items That You Can Find Anywhere, Including Garage Sales, Scrap Metal, and Discarded Items by Eric Michael is yet another goldmine of information on how to make money!

Seriously, whether you want to earn some extra cash in your spare time or want to make a career out of buying and selling, this book (and several others by the same author) will get you going, and keep you there. The appendix is worth the price of the book but every page contains valuable tips and pointers. Highly recommended 5-stars."

5.0 out of 5 stars

This is a great book! It contains lots of ideas on how to make money from surprising places

By **Steven Johnson "Publisher of debt and credit"**

This review is from: Almost Free Money: How to Make Extra Money on Free Items That You Can Find Anywhere, Including Garage Sales, Thrift Shops, Scrap Metal and Finding Gold (Kindle Edition)

"This is a great book! It contains lots of ideas on how to make money from surprising places, and the resource directory at the back of the book is worth 10x the price of this book all by itself. Highly recommended.

I like the way the author told how he got started in this type of business, and his advice on what to sell as scrap, what to sell as collectible, and what to sell as utilitarian, everyday use, was very interesting. I'm sure that as I visit thrift shops and garage sales in the future, this book will help me identify many new items that will make me money!"

Readers' Praise for Eric Michael's Passive Income for Life

5.0 out of 5 stars **A detailed instruction guide for achieving selling success on Amazon** August 5, 2013

By Pete Densmore

"I was hoping this book was going to tell me how to make $50,000 instantly, but I hindsight, I'm very happy it didn't. Because although it's not impossible to make that kind of money quickly, one would either need to be insanely lucky or do something illegal.

Instead, I was pleasantly surprised with Mr. Michael's Passive Income for Life. Like most things in life, making money takes work. It's not something that's handed out on street corners or to those who feel they are entitled. It takes work and it won't happen overnight. That theme is stressed in this book and a theme I will instill with my kids.

Although it will take time, fortunately--with a detailed how-to from Mr. Michael, readers of this book can probably achieve the same success as the author. If they really want it, and if they want to put in the time and effort.

The guidance is real and straight forward. The voice is authentic and compassionate. And the feeling is energetic and positive.

If you're looking for supplemental income, a work from home job or starting your own business, I would highly recommend this book. Online success is achievable, with patience, dedication and drive."

Table of Contents

PREFACE	1
WHY YOU NEED ALMOST FREE GOLD!	4
HOW TO DETERMINE THE VALUE OF GOLD AND PRECIOUS METALS: SPOT PRICES AND PURITIES	7
PREPARING TO BUY GOLD AND SILVER: DEVELOPING YOUR MINDSET AND BUILDING YOUR GOLD KIT	12
IDENTIFYING GOLD, SILVER AND PLATINUM	17
Identifying Precious Metals by Sight – Characteristics of Gold, Silver and Platinum	18
Identifying Precious Metals with Maker's Marks	20
Silver Hallmarks and Silver Makers' Marks	26
Platinum Marks	29
Notes on Silver-Plate and Gold Plated Items	29
Testing Gold and Precious Metals with Test Kits and other Tools	30
LET THE TREASURE HUNT BEGIN: WHERE TO FIND PRECIOUS METALS FOR CHEAP!	33
TIPS FOR FINDING GOLD AND SILVER AT YARD SALES AND GARAGE SALES	42
Tips for Buying Items of Value to Hosts	42
Tips for Finding Hidden Gold and Silver at Yard Sales	45
Which Sales Should You Go to?	46

TREASURE HUNTING FOR GOLD AND SILVER AT THRIFT STORES AND SECOND-HAND STORES	50
Thrift Store Shopping Tips for Prospectors	51
FINDING GOLD AND SILVER AT ANTIQUE SHOPS AND FLEA MARKETS: LOOK FOR SWAG UNDER SPOT PRICE	54
WHERE TO FIND FREE GOLD AND FREE SILVER!	56
PROCESSING VINTAGE ELECTRONICS FOR GOLD AND SILVER CONTENT AND OTHER SOURCES OF CASH	64
HOW TO SELL YOUR GOLD AND SILVER FOR MAXIMUM PROFIT	72
Selling Precious Metals On EBay	76
Refining Your Own Precious Metals	78
TAKING YOUR PRECIOUS METALS BUSINESS TO THE NEXT LEVEL: HOW TO GUARANTEE CONSISTENT SOURCES OF METAL	80
Professional Image	81
Communication and Contact Information	82
Funding	83
Advertising	84
BUSINESSES THAT GENERATE SCRAP PRECIOUS METALS	87
Thrift Stores, Antique Shops and Second-Hand Stores	87
Lost and Founds	88
Dentists, Doctors and Hospitals	89
Jewelers and Jewelry Repair Shops	90
Gold and Silver Manufacturing Shops	91

Auto Shops, Scrap Yards and Car Dealerships	91
Cell Phone, Computer and Electronics Repair Shops	92
ARE GOLD PLATED AND SILVER PLATED ITEMS WORTH BUYING?	94
A SECRET 'NON-PRECIOUS METAL' MORE VALUABLE THAN SILVER?	97
THANK YOU, READERS!	99
WEBSITES AND LINKS	101
RECOMMENDED PAY SITES	105
SOURCES	106
ADDITIONAL RESEARCH	107
ABOUT THE AUTHOR	109

PREFACE

Why do we all love gold?

Yeah, I really asked that question! It's an important question, and the answer is the reason why gold and other precious metals will always be valuable.

It's the reason why men trekked for thousands of miles in terrible conditions during the United States and Canadian gold rushes in the 1800s. It's why Columbus *really* sailed west in 1492. Thousands upon thousands of people have died trying to "strike it rich" with gold.

Gold is the one resource that will always hold value. It is the basis for many country's currencies and the global economy. Gold ain't going out of style. There's a reason why people who are the best in the world in a given athletic competition are given a *gold* medal. Have you ever been told to "go for the nickel"? Was the best example of an item ever called the "copper standard"?

Gold has been the most sought after substance in the world for thousands of years. Humans have been making currency and adornments from gold for centuries. Why, you ask? The properties of gold are the reason that we started using it for countless applications and they are the basis for its value.

- Gold is pretty and shiny (these are not technical terms, I know). It does not tarnish in air, water, or most corrosive chemicals, which has made it an exceptional choice for manufacturing coins, jewelry and decorations since 600 BC. Items made from gold last almost forever and they do not lose their visual appeal.
- Gold is the most malleable metal known to man. It is easy to form it into multiple shapes and forms. It is a very "soft" metal, so it can be used for unlimited purposes. It can be hammered flat. A single ounce of gold can be spread out to over 300 square feet and it can be spread so thin that it becomes transparent. This makes gold valuable in manufacturing electronics, computers, and other high-tech components.
- Gold is heat resistant and it is an exceptional electrical conductor, which also makes it useful in electronics and heat shielding components on vehicles.
- Gold will form alloys with other metals at high temperatures. This is the reason gold is used in amalgam for dental work.

Man has been searching for sources of gold ever since it was discovered almost three thousand years ago, and the novelty has not worn off. The itch to find gold burns brightly today, just like it did for the '49ers in the California Gold Rush.

Even couch 'taters enjoy the search for gold. Who would have thought that a TV show about a small gold claim in Alaska would have gotten so popular? I doubt that even the Discovery Channel thought so many people would be interested in programs like Gold Rush, Alaska and Bring Sea Gold. Yet, the both shows are staples of their current lineup.

Tens of thousands of viewers religiously watch the romantic quest to find gold by other "common men and women". Everybody dreams of finding gold, don't they?

"Goooolllldddd!!!"

WHY YOU NEED ALMOST FREE GOLD!

Now that we have stoked the fire and got the gold fever burning, let's talk about what this book will do for you. Will the book make you instantly rich…? No, but you could very easily find unmarked jewelry worth several thousand dollars after reading this book. You will also learn how to find a large source of free scrap gold, silver and platinum anywhere in the world!

Let's take a brief step back and let me tell you why I am qualified to help you on your quest for treasure.

I began the search for Almost Free Gold over fourteen years ago. I read everything I could get my hands on about methods to find cheap gold, silver and other precious metals as part of my research for my system of selling items and materials that could be located for free and sold online for an excellent source of new income.

I expanded into buying items for extremely affordable prices (mostly under $1) at second-hand locations like thrift shops, yard sales and flea markets. A very important aspect of that system has involved locating precious metals at those locations.

Since the year 2000, I have sold over 10,000 items that I have "picked" from second-hand locations or have found for free while I was recreating. My search for this information and the resulting business plans for developing fun and exciting income sources at very low costs are detailed in #1 Amazon bestsellers Almost Free Money and Passive Income for Life.
I provide fellow pickers and internet sellers over 80 pages of free blog posts on my website at http://www.ericmichaelbooks.com. You can find information on selling a huge array of used items – everything from used media and vintage clothes to scrap metal and everything in between.

I provide this personal resume, if you will, only so that the reader knows where I am coming from when I provide this information. You may be able to find portions of this information (how do you think I learned to do it?) online or in books, but most of this material comes from my personal experiences locating and selling materials and items online. You cannot find most of this information for free, and if you were to try to surf the 'net and put this together, it would take you a very long time.

I have been told that most information providers that sell documents like this book and Almost Free Money charge over $50 for their documents, and actually sell them to customers for that amount. I don't believe in that. I provide this resource to readers for a very affordable charge. In return, all I ask is three things:

1. Leave a positive review on the <u>Amazon book page</u> and on Goodreads.com. The income earned from these books is used for my two boys' college funds.
2. Share this book through your social media outlets and word-of-mouth.
3. Put this information to good use and don't wait to start making money! People who wait for next week usually never end up getting started at all.

Remember, the great thing about Almost Free Gold, Almost Free Money and Passive Income for Life is that as soon as you sell that *first item,* you have already made profit on your book order! Where else can you say that about any investment?

HOW TO DETERMINE THE VALUE OF GOLD AND PRECIOUS METALS: SPOT PRICES AND PURITIES

Before we get to the excitement of hunting for gold and other treasure, we first must learn how to determine the value of the precious metals (PMs) that we will be looking for. In order to get the highest possible profit for each transaction, it is vital to know the current value of the commodity, so that we do not overpay for it in the field.

All metals and commodities that are traded for profit have what is called a 'spot price', which is the market value in the global economy for any security (precious metal) that can be bought for immediate possession at commodities markets.

To give you an idea of current spot prices, at the time this book was written the spot price of gold was $1256 per troy ounce. Platinum was $1356 and silver was $21.

There is a handy precious metal spot price table provided on Kitco.com (http://www.kitco.com/market/). The table shows the major precious metal spots, plus it gives you the AM and PM asking prices, so that you can see if the spot prices are rising, falling, or holding.

The two questions I receive the most often are: 1) What the heck is a troy ounce? 2) Will I get paid at the spot price for gold items that I find?

1) A troy ounce is the traditional measure of weight for gold, and one troy ounce = 1.0971 Oz. There is a troy ounce conversion calculator at http://www.metric-conversions.org/weight/troy-ounces-conversion.htm, which will convert both from troy ounces to standard units and from standard units to troy ounces.

2) No, you will never get paid spot price values for precious metals, including gold. The spot price is the value of pure gold. Once the gold is smelted and formed into jewelry or used for manufacturing anything, the gold is not pure gold anymore. Even 24K gold is not bought at spot price. The spot price only provides a base for negotiating the buy price for precious metals.

So, if we are not going to get paid spot prices, how do we determine the value of particular purities of gold?

Here is the formula for determining the value of gold using current prices:

1. Determine the current gold spot price from the internet. We will use $1256 / per troy ounce for our calculation.
2. Determine price per gram, as that is what most jeweler's scales measure gold in. 1 Troy ounce = 31.1 grams. So, $1256 / 31.1g = $40.39 per gram of gold
3. Separate your gold by purity (K). Weigh your gold, using the scale. Multiply $40.39 x how many grams of gold at each purity. We will start with 14K. For our purposes, we will

say that we have 100 grams of 14K gold. We take $40.39 x 100 and get $4039.
4. Check the conversion table for gold purity and get your adjusted conversion value for 14K gold, which is 0.55. $4039 x 0.5833 = $2221.45.

After our calculation, we know that the value of the gold that we hold in our hands is $2221.45. Rock on!

We have to take into account that we will not earn $2221.45 when we actually sell the gold. This value only gives us the spot price value at the given time, so that we know the value of the gold.

You can expect to receive 90 to 95% of the spot price at a professional assayer or refinery, but you will have a period of time to wait for your payout and many assayers have a minimum weight requirement of three to five ounces of material.

It is possible to receive similar returns (90% or slightly higher) by selling smaller amounts on auction sites such as eBay, but you are at a higher risk, as you are relying on bidding to determine profit. You are able to list at a Buy-it-Now price, but such auctions cost more money and you will still have to pay eBay seller fees after the sale.

It may be tempting to take your gold to a pawn shop or "We Buy Gold" joint, but this is not recommended. You can expect to receive a much lower percentage of your gold's value at these locations. Remember, these places are middle-men. They still have to pay for an assay and then ship out their gold to a refinery. You can expect to receive about 40-70% less than the gold's value at such stores.

An excellent resource to check which companies are paying the most for gold and are the most reliable, http://www.where2sellgold.com has a table that shows value, how fast the companies offered a quote and how quickly they sent gold back to the sender after receiving a return request.

Here is another helpful online calculator for determining the value of gold, depending on purity in karats: http://www.goldcalc.com. It also gives you value of one gram of gold in each purity level – 24k, 14k, etc.

Most professional gold buyers and jewelers adjust the purity values by 3% to account for the common practice of under-karating in the gold jewelry business. The makers of gold jewelry are given an acceptable range that gold jewelry pieces are allowed to test in, so your 10K gold can actually assay at under that value. To account for the variance in the actual gold content in marked gold, you should adjust the purity value by approximately 3%.

Here is a similar calculator / table for sterling silver and silver bullion: http://www.silverrecyclers.com/Calculators/ster_calculator.aspx

Here is a calculator that converts all precious metals to dollar value by each purity and volume for your mobile device / smart phone (very handy to carry with you!) http://gold.yabz.com/mobile.php

If you prefer the actual values for calculating yourself:

Gold

24K = 0.999, Adjusted 0.97

18K = 0.75, Adjusted 0.72

14K = 0.585, Adjusted 0.55

10K = 0.417, Adjusted 0.39

Silver

Fine, Bullion = 0.999

Sterling Silver = 0.925

PREPARING TO BUY GOLD AND SILVER: DEVELOPING YOUR MINDSET AND BUILDING YOUR GOLD KIT

Hey! We're getting closer to the fun stuff, now. We know how to determine how much the treasure that we are going to find is worth, so we can make profit on the items we that we locate.

In this chapter, we are going to get ready to go treasure hunting. We're almost ready to start the quest for…
GOOOOLLLLDDDDD!!!!!

(Sorry. I just get excited, sometimes.)

Anyhow, there are still some things we need to discuss before we go bargain hunting.

The first thing that we have to know before we start buying gold and other precious metals is: What is your buying mindset? Why are you buying precious metals?

There are really three different buying perspectives:

1) Flipping precious metals for immediate profit

2) Buying precious metals as an investment

3) Buying jewelry to wear or to give as gifts

The primary reason that you are looking for gold and silver is going to directly affect how much you are going to be willing to pay. If the only reason you are buying gold is to immediately flip it and sell it to an assayer for 90% of the spot price, your buy price is going to be limited to about 60-70% of the current spot for the purity of the gold, so that you can make enough profit to make the purchase worthwhile.

If, on the other hand, you are buying gold as an investment, you may be willing to offer close to 90% of the spot price, if you are confident that ten years from now, the spot price of gold will be significantly higher than current prices. This is even truer for silver. There are multiple informed sources online that are saying that the price of silver is likely to skyrocket in the next twenty years.

The value of silver is much lower than the value of gold and has been that way forever. There will come a time when silver will become so hard to come by that the spot price will increase dramatically. Silver has a ton of practical uses, in addition to its cosmetic uses. There are estimates that state that over 90% of the silver in the world has already been used in electronics, batteries and other uses and has already been discarded, whereas 95% of gold is retained because of its value. In other words, people do not value silver... yet.

This is awesome for us, as later in this book, we are going to discuss "mining" discarded precious metals, including silver, for profit.

To get back to the point, you should decide ahead of time what you intend to do with the gold and silver that you are going to find. Are you going to flip it, sell it, or keep it?

I started right off with the mindset of buying precious metals as an investment. I have flipped a small percentage of my finds. I remember several years ago, I found a 14K gold class ring for $5 at a garage sale and sold it on eBay in a week for $250. Bam!

My thrill really comes from finding valuable items for free and selling them for profit. I have been collecting gold, silver and platinum from vintage electronics and contacts for years. I have probably fifty pounds of gold and silver-bearing material to be refined and assayed. I also have collected some very nice gold and silver jewelry that I found for free at garage sales or for very cheap at thrift stores. We will discuss how you can do the same thing later.

I also strongly believe that both gold and silver prices will increase dramatically again within the next twenty years, due in part to supply and demand. There is not enough gold coming out of the earth to satisfy future demand, in my opinion. Silver is an even safer bet. When you get a chance to buy silver, I think that you should be saving it as an investment. I have even seen articles that say that the price of silver will surpass the price of gold at some point. Makes you think, doesn't it?

Let's talk for a moment about the historical spot price of gold and silver. The historical price of gold is important to understand (and silver historically parallels the gold price).

The price of gold per ounce stayed fairly constant between $35-40 from 1935 all the way up until 1971, when the US Dollar was removed from the Gold Standard. After 1971, the price of gold jumped from $40 an ounce to $150 an ounce by 1974, and then spiked up to $615 briefly in 1980, before settling back down in the $350-400 range for twenty years.

Do you think there's going to be a difference in how much gold was plated onto costume jewelry, gold rimmed plates, and eyeglass frames in 1968 when gold was $35 an ounce compared to 1995, when gold was $380 dollars an ounce? You betcha.

It wasn't until 2005 that the price of gold really skyrocketed. So, there is still significant gold to be found in items that are not all that old, relatively speaking.

Now, the recent downward trend in gold spot prices gives us an excellent opportunity to find more gold and silver for cheap. In 2012, when the gold spot was almost $2000 a troy ounce, there was a TON of competition for all gold items at second-hand locations. That competition has waned with the falling gold and silver spot price.

Now is an excellent time to look for gold and silver. The prices are lower and there are fewer people looking for it than even several months ago.

So... let's get goin', eh?!

First we have to gather some tools. Here are some tools that you are going to want to have with you when you are looking for gold and silver:

- A gold magnet (I linked to the one I bought – it's a very strong Neodymium magnet that attaches to a key chain.)
- A small magnifying glass or a jeweler's loupe
- A precious metal testing kit (Click on the hyperlink for a portable kit that includes testing for gold, silver, platinum and also a scale and test stone for $16 + shipping.
- A pocket sized Scale that weighs in grams and ounces
- A Pocket Diamond Tester (Only costs $7.60, and works well.)
- A small pair of wire cutters to cut stones from jewelry
- A small flashlight or head lamp for hard to see marks

At the very least you will need a good magnet to see what is underneath the top layer of gold or silver (non-precious metal sticks to a magnet) and a loupe or magnifying glass for seeing tiny karat marks (a lighted loupe is a big bonus). It is better to be prepared and have a field pack prepared than it is to find that "piece of lifetime" for $100 and not be able to test it, thereby missing out on it. Always have your field pack with you. I carry mine in my cargo shorts in the summer, or my wife carries it in her large purse in the winter.

IDENTIFYING GOLD, SILVER AND PLATINUM

We really only have to cover one more subject before we go huntin', but it's very important. It is vital that we positively identify our precious metals so that we can accurately determine their values.

Throughout this chapter, you will see a number of websites referenced and hyperlinked to. I strongly suggest that you navigate to them while you are reading this book the first time, rather than later. That way, you can also bookmark the webpages on your computer browser, so that you can revisit them later.

If you own other titles in the Almost Free Money series, then you are familiar with how I roll. I don't see much need in wasting either my time or yours by rehashing information into this book, when there are excellent resources (with illustrations) that have already been provided to you for free on the internet. You can access those pages from this book using the hyperlinks or cutting-and-pasting the web addresses (URLs) and then you can return to them anytime you need them for reference.

Identifying Precious Metals by Sight – Characteristics of Gold, Silver and Platinum

There are several ways for you to ID precious metals in the field and all of them become easier the more you practice. If you want to get good at finding gold and silver, you should handle the metals and look at them as much as possible. I'm not talking about looking at photos, here. I'm saying, when you see sterling silver items in antique stores… or your in-laws house… or even your own stuff - pick it up, turn it over and feel the surface and the weight of the item. Smell it. Rub it. Become one with the metal, young Jedi.

The more you see and touch silver and gold, the more likely it is going to be that you will spot hidden items at yard sales. You will catch a silver item out of the corner of your and say – "Whoa! That looks like sterling!"

Here are some characteristics of each metal that can help you spot treasure in the field, and let you know that you may have found a gold or silver item at second-hand locations:

GOLD:

- Always has a shiny appearance, only it is very dirty
- Coloration of gold (sounds dumb, but after you see a lot of gold, you can tell the color of karat gold from other similar materials). When karat gold is mixed in with costume jewelry, you can sometimes tell by the difference in the colors

of the gold. Be aware that gold may be alloyed with various metals to make a wide variety of <u>colored gold</u>, including white gold, green gold, pink (rose) gold and red gold.)
- Does not stick to a magnet
- Look to see if there are any areas where the surface has worn off – If there are any other metals showing through under the gold, it is only gold plated.
- Smell – There are gold hunters that swear that they can ID karat gold by the smell alone. I don't think I'd bet the farm on this method, but it's another tool in your kit. I wonder if you could train a dog to locate gold like a police K-9 can find drugs…

STERLING SILVER:

- Tarnishing – Vintage sterling silver decorations often have significant amounts of tarnish on the surface. As a matter of fact, that can work to your advantage. I have found numerous pieces of sterling that stayed on the shelves because they were almost tarnished black and were unsightly.
- Look at the corners and edges of the item for another material showing through (plated)
- Color – Sterling silver is .925 silver. This high silver content makes it appear a lighter silver color than silver-plate, which is composed of mostly copper or aluminum.
- Weight – Silver is denser and heavier than either copper or aluminum. If you find a large silver-colored piece (Be wary at this point. Large sterling items are seldom left out at garage sale prices) and it is fairly light, it is probably silver-plate. Sterling silver items are heavy. They feel substantial

in your hand. One key note: Candlesticks and decorative items often have weighted bases with lead inserts that make them feel very heavy – don't mistake this weight for sterling.
- Texture – High quality silver is very smooth.
- Sound – Sterling makes a clear sound when struck. Lead and aluminum make a dull 'thud'. Copper has a higher tone.
- Does not stick to a magnet (but, copper and aluminum don't stick to a magnet either and they are usually the base metals for silver-plate).

PLATINUM:

- Color – Platinum jewelry is very light colored, a bit lighter than silver. It will not change color with age. It does not tarnish.
- Patina – Pt often develops a sheen, or patina, after it has been worn for a while.
- Weight – Noticeably heavier than gold.

Identifying Precious Metals with Maker's Marks

95% of all karat gold and sterling silver jewelry manufactured after 1906 will be marked with its purity somewhere on the piece. However, these marks are overlooked ALL THE TIME by yard sale hosts, thrift store employees and eBay sellers.

The marks can be tiny. They can be hidden inside rough textures, worn down to the point of being almost unreadable, or the marks may be unfamiliar to the sellers. The more experience that you have looking at jewelry marks, the more likely it will be that you will find those pieces with the marks that others missed.

It also helps a ton to have that experience with the physical characteristics of gold and silver. Mark my words... you will see a piece of jewelry at a yard sale and you will say, "That's sterling. It's gotta be!" The piece will just look and feel like sterling, but you will *not* be able to find the mark. It's happened to me multiple times.

You have to be patient and look at the item in direct light. This is where your lighted loupe can earn its money and find a mark that was missed by many other yard sale flippers. The mark will be there, you just have to find it.

Purity marks for gold items and maker's marks are often stamped on pieces of jewelry in similar locations. While you are conducting your research prior to starting to locate gold, look at as much gold and silver jewelry as you can. Look at new jewelry and antique jewelry and compare and contrast how they are marked. Notice what the marks look like after jewelry has been worn frequently.

After looking at many pieces of jewelry, you will learn where to look for the marks, so that if the mark has been partially rubbed off, you can still see remainders of the marks. This is the #1 source of my "hidden gold" finds at yard sales and thrifts.

I'll give you the list of types of marked jewelry that I find the most often, along with where the pieces are usually stamped:

1. Gold Earrings: The easiest marks to see are usually on the backs, but the original earring backs are often lost or swapped with costume jewelry backs. Most of the 14K earrings that I have found have been located by looking at the tiny marks on the posts of the earrings. These can be tiny and faint and may not be visible except in direct light using magnification. When you start going through earrings, get out your small magnifying glass. Because these marks are so far to see, you can find a lot of gold earrings. They don't weigh much, but it all adds up and they will probably only cost you 25c or so. Earrings are also located quite often because when people lose one earring, they discard the other earring into their costume jewelry pile and it ends up at the yard sale. You can also get quite a few gold earrings by asking yard sale hosts if they have any unmatched gold earrings that they would like to sell.
2. Gold and silver rings and solid bracelets: Rings and solid bracelets are always stamped on the inside of the piece, usually at the bottom for rings. Occasionally, you will see rings stamped underneath the stone in the hollowed-out area. This is a good place to look for pieces that others have missed. If the mark is under the stone, it can be difficult to see. The best way to find hidden gold rings is to look for well-worn rings and then look for a hint of a purity mark. These can be very difficult to see, which is why they are often missed. Look for the characteristics of gold and silver on pieces that show signs of frequent wear. Sometimes, you can catch just a shadow of a mark. I have even bought rings that I suspected to be gold for $1-2, but had no visible marks and then took them home and tested them to confirm that they

were indeed gold. Also, look for rings that have been re-sized, as this often removed a good portion of the purity mark. Another source of cheap gold and silver is class rings. I think that yard sale hosts think that because the rings bear their name and/or school name, that nobody else would want the ring. I have bought several 10K gold class rings for under $5. You can also ask yard sale hosts, "Hey, you have any old class rings that you want some cash for?" Many people don't even think about selling them at their yard sales and usually they don't want them after they are out of school for a couple of years.

3. Gold and silver necklaces, chains and bracelets: Jewelry that has a latch is usually marked on the clasp and also sometimes on a tab that is connected to the clasp. Again, these marks can be tiny on pieces with very small clasps and on children's jewelry. The marked tabs are also frequently lost.

4. Gold and silver charms: These are a great source of hidden gold and silver, because a lot of flippers will look at the bracelet or necklace for marks and then move on. That is where you swoop in and make a score. It is common for people to put marked gold charms on costume jewelry chains or bracelets. Single marked gold and silver charms are regularly received as gifts, and if the recipient doesn't have a fine gold necklace to put them on, they use whatever they already have at home. This is especially true of children's jewelry. I have found 14K gold charms on bracelets that contained 20 other costume jewelry charms and I have also found a number of gold charms on costume jewelry necklaces and even on rope or leather bands. Look for

professional sports logos and zodiac sign charms for sources of real gold and silver. It is also worth noting that vintage charm bracelets and charms can fetch excellent payouts on eBay, even if they are not karat gold or sterling.

5. Gold and silver watches: The marks on watches can be hard to find. Sometimes they are stamped right into the back of the watch on the outside of the watch. But, they can also be stamped inside the back and you have to remove the back of the watch to check it. They can also be marked on clasp of the watch. I have not found a gold or silver watch yet, but I have read that the PM buyers that have found them look for brands of watches and then check them out closer.

It is extremely important that you know what the marks on gold and silver mean, so that you can determine its value.

Gold is usually fairly straightforward. All modern jewelry items over 10K in the US and 9K in Europe are required to be marked somewhere on the piece when the pieces are made.

95% of all fine gold jewelry items found in the US and North America will be plainly marked with their karat designations – 10K (or 10Kt), 14K, 18K, 22K or 24K. One type of mark to look for that is sometimes mistaken for gold plate is a decimal mark, which is used more in Europe. You will sometimes see 14K gold marked '583', 18K marked as '750', and so forth.

Rarely, you also see antique gold jewelry marked as 'Plumb' or with a 'P' after the purity mark. Plumb means that the jewelry contains the exact purity marked on the piece. Sometimes, you will see these gold items marked '14KP' missed, because other buyers think that the 'P' means 'Plated', when it really means 'Plumb'.

You may also see gold jewelry marked 14 KY or 14 KW. The 'Y' and 'W' denote coloration of gold (Yellow and White gold, respectively).

For more details on gold quality marks, see http://www.jewelry-auctioned.com/learn/buying-jewelry/how-to-understand-the-meaning-of-gold-hallmarks.

It is important to understand what some of the other marks on gold jewelry mean. Many cheaper gold-colored pieces and costume jewelry are not pure gold. Instead they are only gold on the extremely thin outside layer of the jewelry.

Filled gold is the most valuable of these types of gold jewelry items. These items are marked 1/10 10K or 1/20 14K, indicating that the gold content is 1/20 gold of 14K purity. In other words, it has some gold content value for larger jewelry pieces like chain necklaces, but there is much less gold than even 10K gold.

Rolled gold is similar to filled gold, with smaller percentages of gold content (must be 1/60 gold). These pieces will be marked 1/60 14K or 1/40 10K, or sometimes just GP or RGP (Rolled Gold Plate)

The jewelry with the smallest percentage of gold is gold plate, or gold electroplate (GE, or HGE for heavy gold electroplate). These pieces have very thin coatings of gold, sometimes only millionths of an inch thick.

Remember that all gold has some value. HGE pieces can net you some profit if you can get them for free or under $1 at a yard sale. For more information on plated gold and a source for buying HGE and filled gold, check out http://www.watchbatterybuyers.com/gold-plated-gold-filled-recycling.php.

Silver Hallmarks and Silver Makers' Marks

Sterling silver items can be much more difficult to identify than their gold counterparts. Sterling is required to be at least .925 silver by weight. Most modern sterling silver jewelry will be marked either 'STERLING', 'STERLING SILVER', 'STER', 'STG', S925, or 925. Rarely, you can find fine silver, which may be marked as 999 or 0.999. You may also see some foreign pieces marked 'Coin Silver', which may also be marked 800 or 900, denoting the 80 to 90% reduced silver content. Some Mexican silver will be marked as such, or have 980 or 950 printed on it with the words 'Taxco Silver'.

Some markings on silver items may indicate items that actually contain no silver at all. Items marked Indian Silver, Mexican Silver, German Silver, Nickel Silver or only 'SILVER' usually are made of a nickel alloy and contain no measurable silver at all.

Occasionally, you will find sterling silver jewelry that has no marks at all. Jewelry made by craftsmen or Native American artists will sometimes contain no makers marks at all to indicate silver content.

For vintage jewelry and larger sterling silver decorative items, silversmiths often printed only a hallmark on the items. The most common of these is the British lion hallmark.

Often, there is no indication besides the hallmark that lets you know that the item is vintage sterling silver. So, it is very important that you review photographs of sterling silver hallmarks on http://www.925-1000.com/ and http://chicagosilver.com/marks_master_list.htm.

Both websites provide many accurate hallmark photographs, so that you can identify the maker of the sterling silver piece. When I am looking for silver at yard sales, I look for hallmarks. Everything marked 'STERLING' will be gone instantly, but occasionally you can find sterling silver items that are marked with only simple hallmarks at yard sale prices (under $5).

Some marks that are labeled as silver, but have very little recoverable metal value are: Silver-plate, Pewter, Silverware, Nickel-plate, Nickel silver and German silver. These alloys either contain no silver at all, or there may be a very thin coating of silver, in the case of silver-plate. It's worth noting here that tableware commonly called silverware really contains no silver at all, although many vintage silverware patterns can fetch more than the silver melt value on eBay and Replacements.com.

Rarely, you will see an item marked 'VERMEIL'. These pieces are mostly sterling silver, covered with gold electroplating. These items have good PM value because of the silver content under the gold plating.

Summary:

These are not a complete list of silver marks, but they are the most common.

Marks that ARE Silver to buy:

'999' '0.999' 'FINE SILVER'

'9854', 'BRITANNIA SILVER', 'CONTINENTAL SILVER', '950'

'STERLING', 'STERLING SILVER', 'STER', 'STG', S925, or 925

'COIN SILVER', 'COIN', 'PURE COIN', 'STANDARD', '900', '850', '835', '800', '750'

'VERMEIL', '925 (Gold colored items)'

The marks 'SILVER' or 'SILVER', followed by a country's name, could mean that the item is silver, but is not high enough purity to be 925 Sterling. If it is silver, it will be 80-90% silver. HOWEVER, there are also countries and makers that mark silver-plate as 'SILVER', so be careful and test it.

Remember, the 3 most common silver marks that you will see: STERLING, STER, 925

Marks that are NOT silver, or are Silver-plate:

'SILVER PLATE', 'STERLING INLAID', 'AFGHAN SILVER', 'NICKEL-PLATE', 'NICKEL SILVER', 'BRITISH SILVER', '1000', 'ARG1000', 'ENGLISH SILVER', 'MEXICAN SILVER', 'SHEFFIELD PLATE', 'OLD SHEFFIELD', 'OLD SHEFFIELD PLATE', 'GERMAN SILVER', 'AUSTRIAN SILVER', 'WOLF SILVER', 'VENETIAN SILVER', 'YUKON SILVER', 'STERLINE', 'EPNS', 'EPWM', 'EPBM', 'EPB', 'EPC', 'EPCA', 'EPGS', 'EPMS', 'AA', 'EP', '18/10', 'SILVERWARE', 'PEWTER'.

Platinum Marks

Platinum and silver are often similar in color, but platinum will be marked 'PLAT', 'PT', and it may also contain a fineness mark, such as 850 PLAT or 800PT. You may also see other alloyed metals listed such as 850PT 150 IRID (for Iridium). For more platinum information:
http://jewelry.about.com/od/platinumjewelry/a/platinum_faq.htm

Notes on Silver-Plate and Gold Plated Items

It's fairly common to find silver and gold plated items for very cheap at yard sales and thrift stores. The question most flippers ask is: Can I make any money from plated gold and silver?

In many cases, you can sell vintage plated gold and silver items as collectibles on eBay and Etsy and make more profit than attempting to sell the pieces for the PM value in the plating, or the scrap metal value of the underlying copper.

As far as the actual metal value of the precious metals, it can vary depending on how old the item is. Older silver-plate like Old Sheffield Plate and HSE can have fairly thick coatings of silver and make it worthwhile to save. Besides, some of them are highly collectible and valuable. Most modern silver-plate is worthless for silver melt value, as the electroplate layer is so thin that it would cost more to strip it off than you would yield in profit from the process.

The thing that we should remember is that often, the silver-plate exterior is covering copper, which you can scrap for about $3/LB at the time that this book was written. If you can find large silver-plate items for pocket change or free at yard sales, by all means, pick them up.

Vintage gold plated decorative items can actually be fairly valuable. I found a 1950s gold covered candy server at a garage sale for $1, and the item yielded over $40 in gold.

Testing Gold and Precious Metals with Test Kits and other Tools

If you want to be absolutely certain that the treasure that you found is gold or platinum, take it to a jeweler and ask them to test it. It may cost you a few bucks, but you will know for sure if it is real.

There are a number of ways to test precious metals at home, or in the field, but there is some judgment involved and you will have to damage your item a bit to test it. This is not an issue if you are buying for scrap gold or silver value, but if you are buying jewelry to wear it or give it as a gift; you may opt to take it to a jeweler.

Here are several methods of testing precious metals, with links to step-by-step instructions:

1) Ceramic plate test – scratch a white plate with a gold object – a real gold object will leave a gold colored scratch in the ceramic. Other gold colored items will make a black mark. Of course, gold plated items will still make a gold streak, so don't use this as your sole method of identifying gold.

2) Electronic gold tester – Electronic devices offer several advantages over acid tests: They are faster -10-15 seconds or so, they are easier to use (with instructions), they are less destructive to the item being tested, the results are easy to understand (LED light indicators or digital readout with more expensive models, and you can use them anywhere. The disadvantages: False positive readings – heavy gold plating will sometimes test as solid gold. Also, the entry level testers have been reported to have given erroneous karat readings (14K reading as 10K on testers, ex.), they are also more expensive than acid test kits (about $90 for a decent model). For directions on how to use an electronic gold tester, here is a helpful YouTube video: http://www.youtube.com/watch?v=SPSFjC2hWCQ

3) Acid Test Kits for Gold, Platinum and Silver – Testing gold and silver with an acid test kit requires the tester to file a small notch in the object and place drops of acid on the metal to determine the purity. This is the most accurate way to test precious metals, but does damage the item a bit, although you can file the notch in an inconspicuous location.

Alternately, you can use a test stone and scrape the jewelry on the stone and then test the scratch with the acid. But again, you will have issues with plated or filled items. Advantages: Relatively accurate, cheaper, tests both gold and silver. Disadvantages: Have to file a notch in the items for best results, have to handle acid, takes longer to perform the test (more intrusive).

Most test kits also contain a platinum acid which reacts with Pt.

Instructions for using an acid test kit:
http://www.ebay.com/gds/How-To-Use-Instructions-Gold-and-Silver-Acid-Test-Kit-/10000000004618603/g.html

YouTube video of a gold item being acid tested:
http://www.youtube.com/watch?v=j93Wj4CF3kQ

LET THE TREASURE HUNT BEGIN: WHERE TO FIND PRECIOUS METALS FOR CHEAP!

Well, now we can start talking about the fun stuff! Let's go find some silver and gold.

      Goooollldddd!!

Ahem. OK. For the next several chapters, we are going to talk about where to find the best deals on precious metals and some tips on how to get gold and silver for well below current spot prices.

We will start by discussing where *not* to go prospecting for gold. Stay away from locations that price their gold and silver using recent spot prices. We can do much better than to go to jewelry stores and pawn shops. These places are going to have gold at the current spot price, or sometimes they will even price items higher than spot price for collectible coins and jewelry. We're going to find some treasure when we go out prospecting, but we don't want to pay retail prices, right?

It's important to set realistic goals for our precious metals business and then make a game plan to achieve those goals. After being out there for years and finding treasure, here are some things that have helped me:

1. Be persistent. You will not find gold or silver at every location that you look. You may not find it every day. But, if you keep looking (especially in the right places), you will find gold and silver. The thrill of the hunt is half of the fun in this business.
2. Realize that there is going to be competition. The days are gone when you would go to yard sales and find a load of silver. Since the gold spot price boom of 2008-2012, there are many people looking for silver and gold. The ads for gold buyers are everywhere. The pressure has been relieved a bit since the spot prices for gold and silver have come down recently, but there are still a lot of people that will be looking for the same treasure that you are.
3. Your best weapon is research. The best way to find more treasure than your competitors is to know more about finding gold and silver than they do. This book is your best weapon. In the coming chapters, you will learn a lot of tricks that will help you find silver and gold provided by gold pickers that have been out there scoring gold and silver paychecks for years. Still, it is very important for you to keep building your knowledge base after reading this book. The <u>EricMichaelBooks</u> blog has evergreen information on finding silver and gold, along with other items that you can resell for good money. You may wish to subscribe to have the new blog posts sent to you via email or RSS. The <u>Almost Free Money Nation</u> also notifies you about upcoming book releases and offers free giveaways. No spam either! There are many other great sites for learning about gold and silver. Keep researching silver hallmarks. Check out the active gold

and silver hunting forums on TreasureNet.com and ScrapMetalJunkie.com for trending discussions.

4. Don't be afraid to talk to people. Ask yard sale hosts if they have any scrap gold or silver that they would like to sell. Talk to your friends and relatives and let them know that you will pay good money for silver and gold. You'd be amazed at how many people have broken gold chains or sterling silver items lying around. Many people are too lazy to take their stuff to gold buyers, or they don't want to deal with people they don't know. These same people are much more likely to sell the items to somebody (you) that they know and trust, especially if you go to their house and get it.

5. Think outside the box. Use your ingenuity to come up with methods of finding gold and silver that other people are not already using. Make up business cards and pass them out to second hand stores. Tell them that you will buy broken sterling silver pieces or broken gold jewelry. That's just one idea that works.

6. Work harder than your competition. Become the guy or gal in your area that people know to call to sell their scrap precious metals. When you go prospecting, start early and hit a lot of sales fast. Learn how to process a yard sale or second-hand store efficiently, but productively. There are many free tips about processing yard sales and thrift stores in my blog.

7. Diversify. Learn about other materials and items that you can find while you are looking for gold and silver and sell online. There are many items that you can find for free that will earn you more money than scrap silver! Look for these items while you are looking for precious metals. I have

found hundreds of books, records and collectibles for free or for quarters and sold them for up to $250. It really helps the bottom line to have other stuff to look for when the precious metals are hard to come by. It's also great to have a list of stuff that you know that you can instantly turn around for profit. Items like cell phones and rechargeable batteries can often be found for free and sent to online buyers for instant cash. Check out the appendix lists in <u>Almost Free Money</u> for over 500 items that can be found for free and sold for good money.

Before we go about setting up our blueprint for successful treasure hunting, let's discuss our options for treasure hunting locations that will yield gold and silver, without paying premium prices.

In subsequent chapters, we will go more in-depth and talk about how to find gold and silver at each of these locations. We will also discuss how to find great treasure others shoppers have missed.

<u>Yard Sales, Garage Sales and Estate Sales</u>

ADVANTAGES:

- Prices – Will have the cheapest average prices for gold and silver items
- Potential for HUGE steals – These places are BY FAR the best chance to find karat gold and large sterling silver items for under $10.
- These people are looking for a quick buck. Often, they are also selling other people's stuff. Usually, they don't know

much about gold and silver. They sure don't know what current spot prices are. In other words, yard sale hosts want to sell stuff fast and sometimes they don't know (or don't care) about their precious metal items' values.
- This can also be a disadvantage, too. Often, silver (and sometimes gold) items are not identified as such. It is very possible to find these items inside boxes of crap or jumbled in with costume jewelry. The host often does not know what they have, especially for items that are not clearly marked as gold or silver on the pieces.
- The potential for multiple finds in one spot. If you get lucky and find a sale that has a bunch of jewelry for sale or sterling silver pieces, there is a good chance that there are multiple items for you to buy.

DISADVANTAGES:

- Competition – Sales are usually only 1-2 days long, so the sales that are advertised as having precious metals or jewelry may have many buyers competing for a few good pieces. Most of the good stuff will be gone instantly.
- They are on the weekends. This can interfere with your personal and family recreational plans on your days off, if you work a 9-5 job.
- Better be there early! Your competition will start at 6AM, waiting in their crappy cars in front of closed sales, or even bothering hosts and knocking on their doors asking for early sales. I hate these people, but it's important to realize that they are out there. I am not one of those people.
- You may get dirty. Bring your hand sanitizer. Some garage sales are dirty and stinky. You might have to dig through

boxes of nasty stuff to find treasure. Some of my best finds have been at trailers.
- You might have to haggle. Some gold and silver buyers don't like this, but if you are going to be successful, you had better get used it. Often, hosts are lazy or they are so clueless that they have no idea how to price gold and silver. The result? There's no price on the items, or a 'Make Offer' sticker. Be ready to deal, and offer way under the spot price.

Thrift Stores and Second-Hand Stores

ADVANTAGES:

- Large inventory. It can be like having 100 yard sales in one location.
- Save money on gas costs by hitting two or three thrift stores, instead of 50 garage sales.
- The people that price the goods often don't know much about precious metals. They don't get a percentage of the sales, either.
- The larger thrifts are open 7 days a week and often open until 7PM.
- Most take credit cards and they usually accept personal checks.

DISADVANTAGES:

- Competition –Precious metals buyers hit large chain thrifts regularly
- Prices are usually higher than yard sales

- Some stores are so large that it is hard to find the treasure within the piles of junk on the shelves.

Antique Shops

ADVANTAGES:

- Can be hidden gems and sources of multiple sterling silver finds for well under spot price.
- Small antique shops are usually willing to negotiate on prices
- Prices are often set on silver items and jewelry and then placed on shelves or inside cases. They are seldom adjusted for current spot prices.
- It is possible to get really good deals on tarnished sterling silver items or dented and damaged items.
- You can get to know the owners / managers and have them call you when PM items come in.

DISADVANTAGES:

- Precious metal items are often priced based on spot prices, or even worse, using collectibles price guides.
- Smaller shops may have odd hours or may even close for the winter.

Flea Markets

ADVANTAGES:

- Can be lots of PM items at large flea markets
- Dealers will almost always make a deal on the price

DISADVANTAGES:

- Premium pricing from many vendors
- Potential for counterfeit items and scams
- Can have odd hours or only open certain weekends
- Wide range of pricing. Most vendors use spot prices to price items.

Family and Friends

ADVANTAGES:

- You have the advantage of being trusted and the seller already likes you.
- Seller more willing to dig items out from storage for a friend/relative.
- Can get items for relatively cheap.
- Network. Tell your friends that you can help them out by giving them money for scrap gold and silver based on current spot prices. Your friends will also tell their family and friends. There are many people who need money from time to time and you can help them out by buying items they don't use anyways.

DISADVANTAGES:

- Make sure you give your friends and family offers near spot price – don't be tempted to accept low prices offered those friends who don't know the value of gold, silver. Make your friends and family fair offers.
- Can be hard to ask about keepsakes, if you know the people.

Metal Detecting

ADVANTAGES:

- A very fun way to look for gold. You might as well have a hobby that pays you, instead of paying big bucks for playing golf.
- Potential to find large ticket items like $5000 engagement rings that were lost at the beach.

DISADVANTAGES:

- High initial expense – good metal detectors cost over $800
- Low time spent to profit ratio.
- You may never find any significant gold or silver
- Takes time to learn

TIPS FOR FINDING GOLD AND SILVER AT YARD SALES AND GARAGE SALES

I have found much more gold and silver at yard sales than anywhere else. There is no better place to find precious metals for cheap (and free in some cases).

Now, there are two very different categories of garage sale treasure; the stuff that the host knows is valuable and the stuff that they don't understand is valuable at all. The manner in which you acquire the two categories of precious metals is going to require totally different approaches. A simple glance at the price tag and noting where the item is displayed at the sale will tell you if they know what it is worth.

Items that the host thinks are valuable will be prominently displayed near the pay table, so they can keep an eye on them. Don't want somebody to steal the good stuff, you know! The hosts' valuables and collectibles will also usually be on the same table and they will be at the front of the display area, so customers can easily find them.

Tips for Buying Items of Value to Hosts

- These items are going to be higher priced, so you have to be able to determine value, using your precious metal calculators with current spot prices. You must be able to make a fair offer and still have room for profit.

- The sticker price is almost never the final price. Establish a rapport with the host and then work your way into asking if their price on their sterling coffee pot is negotiable. Do not insult hosts by offering a low-ball price! Remember, these pieces are likely to have sentimental value and the host is only selling them out of necessity. Make a deal that makes you both happy.
- After you find a great piece, don't rush to the pay table. Pick the item up and look for more swag. Chances are pretty good that if they have one piece, they probably have more available. If you can find multiple pieces, you can usually get a great price by bundling them and offering to buy all of the PM items at one low price.
- After you make a deal, ask the host if they have any more silver or gold to sell – "Man, I even take busted scrap jewelry and unmatched earrings, if they are marked." Many people are surprised that scrap pieces are worth anything.
- Carry business cards. If the host won't come down on an overpriced item, tell them to call you or text, and you'll come back and buy the item at the price offered, if it does not sell. You would be surprised how often this works.
- Make sure that you have enough cash to buy a great item, if you find it. This is vital! You can always put the cash back in your bank account later and you do not have to carry the money at the sale, on your person. You can lock it in your vehicle. The last thing that you want to have happen is this scenario: You find a gold wedding ring worth $1000 and the host just wants it gone after she recently got divorced, so she

has $200 on it. You ask if she will take $100, because that is all the cash that you have on you. She says no. You ask if she will hold it for you, while you go get the rest of the cash. She says no. Guess what happens when you leave to get the other $100. Yep, gone! $800 lost.

- Most hosts value marked karat gold jewelry. But, it is easier to find sterling silver decorative items for reasonable prices. Silver jewelry is also easier to buy.
- This works awesome… identify a piece that you really like that's under the metal's spot price. Then, pick out a second piece that is obviously the hosts' favorite item – it will be overpriced and at the front of the display area. Make an offer on the overpriced item that you know that the host will not accept. When he or she says no, act like you are disappointed and say, "Oh…OK. Well… would you take $X for this other little ring over here?" This works 9 times out of 10. You have to be an actor or actress sometimes to get good deals.

Now we will get to the really fun stuff – finding hidden gold and silver for almost nothing. There is nothing quite like finding karat gold jewelry hidden amongst a bunch of junk. It's like walking down the street and seeing a $100 bill lying on the ground.

The thing that we have to keep in mind here is that if the host knew it was valuable, it would be displayed more prominently. Also, unless you were at the sale in the first few minutes, these bargains would have been picked up by another shopper, right?

So, where do we look for these hidden treasures, you ask?

Gold and silver can be anywhere! The more you look for it and find it, the better you will get at finding additional pieces. Once you get the "Golden Eye", the stuff will find *you*. It's not luck that a few people find 80% of the gold and sterling silver at second-hand locations. They are the best and most experienced at what they do.

So, what do these experienced buyers do that most others don't?

Tips for Finding Hidden Gold and Silver at Yard Sales

- Look inside...EVERYTHING. The swag can be hiding anywhere. I have found hidden treasure inside boxes of junk, in free boxes, inside locked lockboxes for 25c (pried it open later), inside board games boxes, in cologne and perfume boxes, inside toys, in the pockets of jackets, and many other weird locations.
- Look in storage boxes that are under tables. Search boxes all the way to the bottom and be thorough.
- ALWAYS look inside bags of costume jewelry. I have bought large bags of costume junk for $1 or less and then dug through it later and found some nice pieces. You can always make your $1 back by selling the costume jewelry on eBay. Some vintage costume jewelry is actually quite valuable on its own.
- Look for gold marks very carefully in direct sunlight, if possible. It is common for sellers to overlook marks on 14K jewelry that is marked on the posts of earrings, inside clasps, on the rough edges, etc. I have also seen items that I thought

looked like karat gold, but I could not find a mark on them. I bought it for a quarter, just in case, then later got it home and found karat marks. Bang!
- Look very closely for silver items that are marked with only maker's marks or hallmarks. Most yard sale resellers know to buy silver marked 'STERLING' or 'STER'. They know the British lion sterling silver hallmark. You can find some great pieces that have more obscure sterling silver marks. Spend time studying these marks, so you know them when you see them. And, when in doubt, buy it, if it has a mark that might be sterling silver. The worst that could happen is that you have to sell the item as vintage silver-plate on eBay. The potential for a big score is worth the chance of losing a couple of bucks on silver-plate look-alikes.
- Look for less common gold marks, as discussed earlier – ex. 14K gold marked '.585'. You can also find rolled gold and heavy electroplate (HGE) for pocket change, sometimes. These items are worth buying, if you can get them for cheap.

Which Sales Should You Go to?

It's very important that you maximize your efforts on garage sale days. Remember, you only have *at most* an hour or two of prime picking time at the beginning of yard sales on Friday and Saturday. So, how do you decide which sales to hit first during the "golden hours" between 7-9AM, or so?

On Thursday, check all of the classified listings in your area for garage sales. Many people list their sales on Craigslist, but some senior citizens still do things the old-fashioned way and list only in "Super Shopper" type circulars or in the classifieds in their local newspapers. The sales that are listed only in newspapers can be a great source of PMs, as older sale hosts are more likely to have a collection of jewelry at their sales.

First, write down the sales that are *not* on internet listings. Look at those listings and pick out one or two that appear to have an accumulation of goods for sale. Hopefully one or two of them are sales that start between 7-8AM.

Next, check out the internet yard sale listings. Watch out for people that hold yard sales every week and eBay sellers trying to unload their unsold inventory. Some antique dealers and thrift store owners also hold yard sales several times a month. We would prefer to not spend our "golden hours" on those locations, as they know the value of PMs.

Think about what types of words you would use if you were a professional seller trying to make your yard sale sound good to flippers. You will see many of these people using phrases like: "1st sale in 20 years!", "lots of vintage collectibles", "collectible toys", "high value antiques", or anything similar that would attract resellers.

What are some of the phrases that we want to see in yard sale listings? I look for the following: Multiple family sales, lots of knick-knacks (many are sterling), curios, coin collections, records (because these are mostly older hosts that will have other valuables), and other items older than 25 years old listed without calling them "vintage" or "antique".

Another thing to look for is lazy people's listings. Why?

Well for starters, you will have a lot less competition at these sales. The sales don't advertise gold, silver or collectibles, so you won't have pickers and flippers there. Another reason to go to these sales is, well… these people obviously don't care about making money at their sale, or they would make more of an effort to get customers to go to their sale. These type of people are much more likely to have missed karat gold and sterling silver items when they list their stuff. They are also the type to just throw a bunch of jewelry in a bag and list for $1, instead of going through it first to see if there 14K gold in there.

You get my point. Finding lazy people's yard sales should be priority #1. Another excellent way to find these hidden gold mines is to keep your eyes peeled while you are en route to sales on your list. If you pass a little brown cardboard sign with a crappy looking arrow and only the word 'SALE' on it, head there immediately. Any sales that are not advertised can be great sources of swag.

You can also find some great stuff at sales during the week. Occasionally, you will see sales that start on Wednesday or Thursday. That same is true of estate sales and inside sales during the winter in cold climates. There is much less competition at these sales. You can also pick up some great stuff by yard sale shopping when it is cold or rainy. Be tougher than your competition. Some sales will be canceled due to the weather, but many will just slide more stuff into the garage where it is warm and dry.

For many free general garage sale shopping tips, check out: http://garagesaleacademy.com/garage-sale-shopping-bargains/

For tips on diversifying into other yard sale treasures to sell, please see: http://www.ericmichaelbooks.com/blog/top-10-money-making-garage-sale-items

TREASURE HUNTING FOR GOLD AND SILVER AT THRIFT STORES AND SECOND-HAND STORES

Gold and silver can be found at thrift stores anywhere in the world. The trick is to find the best stores and then learn how to find the hidden treasures amongst the piles of worthless junk at most of these stores.

In metropolitan areas, it can be really tough to find precious metals in the large chain thrifts like Goodwill and Salvation Army, as these locations are routinely picked through by the professional gold and silver buyers. Still, you can find some good stuff, especially if you know what to look for in sterling silver.

I think that the most important thing to accomplish is to find some of the smaller, out-of-the-way thrift shops and start visiting them at various times. Get a feel for how often they receive gold and silver items and how they price them. These types of shops usually get fewer visitors and they are hit less often by the pros.

In urban areas, this may mean driving a bit further from downtown or going to some less affluent areas, but you can really find some good swag if you find good sources of second-hand gold that are priced to sell.

In most second-hand shops, you are not going to find marked gold and sterling silver at garage sale prices. Unless you are "Johnny-on-the-spot" when the item hits the shelf, even if employees miss the gold marks, somebody else will scarf them up lickety-split.

So, you are going to be looking for two things: Marked precious metals priced below spot price and hidden gems. I have found significant amounts of both types of swag at almost every thrift store that I go prospecting in.

Thrift Store Shopping Tips for Prospectors

- Most of the marked gold and silver items will be within sight of the pay counter or in a locked glass cabinet under the registers. Start there. Make sure that you have your scale and calculator to check if the item is under spot price.
- If you only remember one tip about thrifting, remember this: I have found by far the most sterling silver and some vermeil (gold-plated sterling) inside bags of junk silver colored objects. The best area is in the tableware and serving sections. I have found some large sterling pieces in bags of silverware. Plus, as I mentioned before, even vintage non-sterling silverware can be valuable, sometimes worth as much as the silver content of sterling items – Here is a free blog post about selling vintage silverware: http://www.ericmichaelbooks.com/blog/selling-silverware-for-profit.

- Talk to the clerks, especially if they are not at a register. Ask the employees that are stocking shelves if they have any silver or gold in back that has not been brought out yet. What's the worst that could happen? They tell you no, or they can't tell you whether they do or not. It never hurts to ask. You might get lucky.
- Again, look for obscure hallmarks and hidden marks.
- Look for dented silver items. Silver plate does not dent easily. Sterling does.
- Pick up EVERYTHING that might be sterling and check the mark. You will pick up probably fifty silver-plate items for every sterling item, but it's worth it. It only takes a second to check an item for sterling marks.
- Look for dark colored or tarnished silver. Some will be thick silver-plate, but occasionally you will find sterling.
- Some sterling items that I have found on shelves at thrifts: Serving tongs, serving spoons, tableware, picture frames, souvenir spoons, thimbles, buttons, jewelry, letter openers, salt and pepper shakers, vases, serving bowls, platters, bookmarks, pens, candlesticks, curios, Christmas ornaments and decorations (another good source of regularly missed silver), wine stoppers – those are just a few that I can think of right now.
- Go thrifting a lot. You never know when that sterling candlestick will hit the shelves (unless you have made an inside connection). You have to be there to buy it. The good stuff does not stay on the shelf for long.
- Try to figure out if there are days when the thrift stores do a lot of shelf stocking. The obvious day to be out thrifting is on Monday. Lots of people drop off stuff over the weekends or

Monday morning after weekend garage sales. Also, some stores have employees stocking shelves on weekends when they are closed.

For more free tips on thrift store flipping, see
http://www.ericmichaelbooks.com/blog/thrift-shop-flipping

FINDING GOLD AND SILVER AT ANTIQUE SHOPS AND FLEA MARKETS: LOOK FOR SWAG UNDER SPOT PRICE

It is possible to find some good gold and silver items at flea markets and antique shops, but you probably are not going to find many real steals like you can find at yard sales and thrift stores.

Remember, most of the people that own antique stores know their stuff. Most flea market vendors are flippers, just like you. They know what precious metal items are worth – more or less.

There is going to be some items that can make you some money and you may find a great item every once in a while at a flea market, but the chances are significantly less than at the other locations. The people that run flea market booths and antique shops are out to make money for themselves. They usually do not have employees pricing their precious metal items, like thrift stores do.

So, what are we looking for at these locations? Usually you can find some good pieces with room for profit under current spot prices, especially if the spot prices have risen within several months of your shopping trip.

As we discussed earlier, most items are priced at these locations and they are not adjusted very often. Many expensive silver and gold items may sit in their shop or booth for a while, especially in small towns or stores that don't get a lot of shoppers.

When you shop at these places, look for the items that appear to have been in the shop for a while. Often, they are dusty or have been placed high on shelves or behind other items. Look for slightly damaged or dented silver items.

Many flea market vendors will deal with you. They are always looking for a quick deal, as long as they are making profit over the price that they bought the item for (usually from a yard sale). Don't be afraid to offer low-ball prices to flea market vendors. They have no emotional attachments to the items, in most cases.

Don't be afraid to look for unmarked pieces at these locations. It is very possible to find a small antique shop or individual antique vendor in an antique mall that undervalues sterling silver or even misses hallmarks. If you study your silver hallmarks, you can find some valuable large sterling pieces at antique shops. You can also find small decorative items and serving ware that have been overlooked.

Similarly, the experience and professionalism of flea market vendors can vary greatly, so do some looking around and figure out which vendors sell undervalued or overlooked PMs at their booths and frequent them often.

WHERE TO FIND FREE GOLD AND FREE SILVER!

*Portions reprinted from the book Almost Free Money

We all know about the traditional methods of finding gold, including strip mining, gold panning, and dredging. All of them involve back-breaking labor and lots of money invested in order to get a small amount of gold.

Why go through all this effort when there is gold to be found above ground for very little cost, or for free? Let's talk about some specific items that you can find at garage sales, thrift stores, and in junk piles that can add to your bottom line.

The PRIME decade for finding the most gold and silver in scrap electronics and decorations is from about 1961 to 1971. This is the time period when gold and silver had the most uses, and electronics from the era were often heavily plated with silver, and sometimes gold. Manufacturers were much more lenient in the application of gold and silver - remember, gold was only $35 an ounce, compared to over $1200 an ounce today.

It is common to find electronics from the 1960s for next to nothing at garage sales, thrift stores, or even laying in junk heaps. I guarantee you that there are thousands of these items in landfills near you right now. The electronics from the 60s are now over fifty years old – most items are broken, missing pieces, or downright outdated. A few are collector's items, but most are heavy, bulky clunkers that take up too much room in people's homes.

I want to take a second here to let you know that all of the components and locations that I will be discussing are illustrated in great detail on Scrap Metal Junkie and in the Scribd link provided at the end of this book. You may wish to open up internet browser tabs for both of these sites, so that you can take a look at the photos as you are reading this book.

You can also find gold and silver within the metal appliances and electronic scrap that you find discarded in various locations. This is where you can really make some extra dough. Silver currently spots at over $20 a troy ounce and gold sells for over $1200 a troy ounce. It does not take much gold or silver to make some nice quick cash.

Where can I find this gold and silver, you may ask?

Ah... that is question, isn't it? There is a ton of information on locating scrap silver and gold on the internet. The Scrap Metal Junkie forums are an exceptional source of information on scrapping vintage electronics for PM value.

To make a long story short, there are several locations where you can consistently find silver and gold in electronics and machinery. Computers have a fair amount of gold in the fingers on the connectors of the circuit boards, and also within the CPU processor chips. The older the computer is, the higher the gold content they have inside them, in most cases. Some of the older circuit boards are actually gold plated.

Another good place to find silver and gold is in electrical contacts. While these contacts are often small and worth only 25 cents to a dollar, some silver contacts in vintage industrial machinery can be worth $20 a piece. I have found silver contacts in 1950s industrial lifts that weighed almost two ounces, or about $50 a piece!

This can be to your advantage, because a lot of the free electronics and machinery you are going to find will be rusty old items. It is quite common to find 1950s or 60s electrical junk laying there in the woods, just waiting for you to take it home and disassemble it for free gold and silver!

Some other common places to find gold and silver is in thin interior wires in vintage electronics, some gold faced diodes in computers, vintage rotary telephone and telecommunications items, vintage video game systems, and inside cellular telephones.

I have found hundreds of dollars' worth of gold and silver just lying around in the woods and in junk piles, just waiting to be reclaimed. Does it have the romance of panning for gold in a mountain stream in Alaska? No, it doesn't. But the value is the same - gold is gold, plain and simple. It's not worth less, just because the gold is inside electronics, instead of being used to make gold jewelry or coins.

What is most important in locating gold and silver is to understand where it has been used. This is accomplished through diligent research, including the reading of this book. Remember, it does not take much gold or silver material (grams and ounces, not pounds) to add up to significant profits.

If you can collect enough gold plated items or gold contacts to add up to one troy ounce of gold, then you have "mined" enough material to equal seven or eight large truck-loads of scrap steel!

First of all, look for scrap or discarded computers from the 1980s and 90s. You can find these computers for next to nothing. I have found quite a few computers in free boxes at sales and lying in the woods. They all have gold, silver and platinum inside them, it is only a question of how much there is.

First, almost all motherboards contain gold in the connector fingers. Motherboards are the main circuit board inside the computer, and they will also have a heat sink with an IC chip underneath. The IC chip will also contain a significant amount of gold, and sometimes these IC chips can be worth more than the spot gold value because of the collectible market of these chips to 'techies'. Check your eBay completed listings to see if the IC chip is worth more as a collectible piece before you scrap it.

Some of the older personal computers can have circuit boards that are completely lined with plated gold, and many of the connectors within the circuit boards also contain gold. Communications devices and high-tech items from the 1980s can also contain similar boards.

The circuit boards inside back planes and hard drives in computers also contain gold and silver in small amounts. These items are often more valuable sold as whole units, instead of disassembling them into smaller parts.

The same is also true of RAM, or computer memory boards, which also contain small gold fingers. RAM is almost always more valuable when sold as whole boards than they are after the gold fingers have been trimmed off of the boards. The smaller wires and the connector jacks that connect the wires to the circuit boards also often have gold or silver inside them.

Platinum can also be found in minute amounts in the platters of hard drives inside computers. These items can be saved and sold in large lots.

Gold can be found inside of every cellular telephone. Some of the early cell phones had a significant amount of gold in their circuitry, and these are the phones that you can find in junk piles and free boxes. All cell phones are worth money. If you see them, pick them up. If nothing else, there are many internet sites that offer a set price for scrap phones, dead or alive, so they are worth your time to pick them up.

Newer printer cartridges also contain gold in their contact buttons, which is why they also have a set scrap value on a number of internet sites.

There are many vintage items from the 60s and 70s that actually contain a fair amount of gold. Almost every item with a circuit board has gold or silver contacts. Some of the high-end electronics have large gold contacts. I once found a large factory loader from the 1960s that had interior gold contacts that added up to over ¼ ounce of pure gold, which is worth over $350 in today's gold market!

I have found that 1960s audio equipment, including turntables, consoles, and radios will occasionally have silver coated copper wires throughout the entire main circuit board. These wires are always worth saving for precious metal refining. All of these vintage audio items have gold and silver contacts, and they also have a fair amount of copper wiring inside them.

Rotary telephones from the 1960s - early 1980s contain gold in their mouth pieces, and in several other internal contacts. The jacks of virtually all telephones contain small amounts of gold inside the connectors.

There also many vintage items that you can find small amounts of plated gold in, where you would not expect to find any gold at all.

Such items would include: Some cologne and perfume caps, designer pens and pen holders, older trophies, dental work, lamps and lamp shades, gold colored trim in band uniforms and Rotary and Lions Club hats, Gold-trimmed china and dishes, picture frames, purse trim, lapel pins, clocks, cigarette holders, cuff-links, eyeglass frames, plaques, emblems, calculators, all switches, plug ends, telephone key pads, ribbon connectors, thermostatic contacts from high temperature items like popcorn poppers and electric skillets, coasters, waste baskets, vintage clothes with gold-colored trim, coffee cups, and many more locations. If the item looks like it may possibly be gold, test it with your gold tester!

This subject is expanded on at one of our most popular pages titled <u>Finding Gold and Silver</u> on ericmichaelbooks.com.

1950s and 60s gold-colored lamps are fairly easy to find in thrift stores, as they are large by today's standards and therefore sell slowly. Some of the these large lamps have a fair amount of gold plating in their bases, well worth the asking price at thrift stores, which is often $1-2.

There are many places that you can find items with interior components that you can sell, or scrap for metal value. You just have to use some ingenuity.

Besides finding items set out for free or discarded in the woods, you can also get these items for free by doing some leg-work. Think about where these items are going to show up.

Where do items that do not sell at garage sales go when the sales wrap up? In the garbage? Why not make yourself some business cards and give them to garage sales hosts. Tell them that you will haul away all their unsold items for free after the sale ends? You are going to get some junk, and you may need access to a dumpster, but you will get a lot of good scrap metal and other PM items that we have discussed. For large sales, you may even get paid a nominal fee just to haul the junk away!

You can also make a classified ad or Craig's List ad that offers your services for removal of appliances, electronics and other items.

You could visit second-hand stores and antique shops and ask the manager if you could leave a large box for them to put broken or unsold vintage electronics, gold and silver plated items, etc. You may have to pay a small fee for each box-full of items, but you probably won't. Start thinking about where dead electronics and appliances may be found, and you will come up more ideas on your own.

PROCESSING VINTAGE ELECTRONICS FOR GOLD AND SILVER CONTENT AND OTHER SOURCES OF CASH

*Portions reprinted from the book Almost Free Money

As we have discussed in prior chapters, there are many ways to find free gold and silver anywhere in the world. The payout will not be as high as finding karat gold or sterling silver, because the precious metals are present in much smaller amounts.

However, this is a *free* source of precious metals! I find it amazing that prospectors will travel across the country to pan for gold or hunt gold nuggets with metal detectors and then scoff at their fellow gold hunters that dig it out of junk electronics and computers.

I say that the electronics miner is the smarter and more fiscally responsible of the two examples given. The gold panner and nuggeteer has a very good chance of spending a lot of time and gas money and finding ZERO gold, while the electronics miner will find gold, silver, platinum, or all three metals EVERY TIME HE TAKES APART VINTAGE ELECTRONICS and he has no costs to worry about. As long as you don't mind spending some time breaking stuff and taking apart machinery, you can find precious metals for free.

Yeah. That's right. Almost every piece of vintage electronics has gold and silver contacts. Some have larger contacts than others, but they all have them. Many electronics also contain a fair amount of other semi-precious scrap metals like copper, brass and shiny aluminum that can also add up quickly.

It is important that you do some research before you start processing electronics and computers for scrap value. There are several things that you will want to research BEFORE you take apart any vintage electronic item.

As we discussed before, you should research Completed Items on eBay, and determine which components are worth selling whole. Again, you should know ahead of time which assemblies are better sold whole, and which assemblies should be broken down into even smaller components, or individual parts.

Once you have an idea of which parts you will be removing for sale, take your item to a location where you can make a mess, but not lose any small parts. A large table top or work bench works well.

Gather your tools. The tools you will use most often are: both types of screwdrivers, needle-nose pliers, wire cutters, an adjustable wrench, a hammer, a magnet, several large vinyl trash bags, and safety glasses and gloves.

You can expedite the process with a cordless drill or power screwdriver with both driver bits. A power rotary tool (Dremel) with a supply of cut-off disks and a drill bit is well worth the investment, if you do not have one. I use mine constantly.

You may also need a set of sockets, and you will occasionally find exotic screw heads like star bits and Allen wrench heads, but if you have a Dremel, you can cut off the screws, or make them into standard screwdriver heads by slicing them with the cut-off disk. You will also use the Dremel for cutting off rusted or stripped screws and bolts. It cuts through thick copper cord insulation like butter, saving you tons of time!

Please heed a word of caution. Before you start breaking stuff, make sure you know what you are doing. Remember, in the 1950s and 60s, nobody even knew what a 'health code violation' was. Old electronics and appliances can contain some nasty stuff. There is mercury inside some old glass switches and components, for instance. You should not open anything that is sealed in glass, or welded shut, unless you know for sure what is inside.

OK, now that we got that out of the way, let's break some stuff. Start on the outside and CAREFULLY remove any decorative items, advertising badges, knobs, feet, etc., that you can sell. Remember, the plastic is going to be old and brittle on vintage items. If you snap the emblem in half, it is worthless. Believe me, I have broken some, even though I was being very careful. Even the glass in the display covers is more brittle in many older components.

After the outer pieces are removed, check eBay Completed Listings to see if the outer shell of your item can be sold. Often, the shells and cases of audio components, and even rotary telephones can be sold.

I usually start by using the cordless drill and unscrewing all of the screws that I can see on the outside of the device. Remove the outer shell, or the access panel to get at the interior of the item. If the shell is going to be sold, put it in your 'Sell' pile. If it is not going to be sold and it is plastic, throw it in your trash bag. If it is metal, hit it with a magnet. If it is ferrous, throw it in your 'Steel' pile. Sometimes the shell will be aluminum and should be saved in its own pile with other aluminum.

I save all of my screws, bolts and other connectors, as well. I put them all in a large coffee can. When it's full, I intend to sell the lot on eBay in the vintage electronics category for about $20. I also sometimes use various screws when I need them for household repairs, or sometimes screws are sold with components, and I need to replace a couple that I lost. Occasionally, you will find screws and bolts made of solid brass or aluminum. Save these in their respective scrap pile.

Now that you are into the interior of the item, find the components that you are looking to sell, and remove them. Put them in your Sell pile. Save the screws and attachments for the items that you are going to sell if possible and sell them with the component. If you lose a screw, don't worry about it. The screws are just for insurance, in case the buyer needs them. They are not required.

Try to avoid clipping wires connected to components that you plan to sell. Carefully pull wires that have jacks or plugs from their ports using needle-nose pliers. Remember, your buyer is going to be hooking the component into his or her system, and is not going to want to splice wires, if it is avoidable.

If there are multiple components available to buy on eBay, and some of the listings have the entire wires, with the plugs, and yours have clipped ends, your item will not get many bids, or it will not sell if it is a fixed price auction.

Once all of your sellable components have been removed, the fun starts. Take one last look, and see if there might be anything else that you could sell that you did not find on eBay before. When you are satisfied that everything that could be sold has been removed, you are ready to start scrapping.

You should realize that there are also whole components that can be sold as scrap, on eBay, via an E-Scrap website, or at your local scrap yard. Internet sites such as Boardsort.com offer fixed prices for items such as computer hard drives, circuit boards, cellular telephones, and computer power supply boxes. You should check these sites so that you know what you will be saving, and the prices that are offered. Several of these sites are listed in the appendices of this document, with hyperlinks to their websites.

Now that you know what you are looking for, get out your USPS Priority Mail Flat Rate Boxes. Label the boxes with the materials that you intend to place in them. In addition, you will need extra-large boxes or totes for ferrous steel, and medium and low class circuit boards. You will have a lot of these materials.

I normally collect a fair amount of vintage electronics and appliance parts before I have a disassembly session, so that I can get a lot of scrap to sell at one time.

When I start scrapping, I always have the following Large Flat Rate boxes ready for material collection: Bare Copper, Insulated Copper, Bare Brass (It is OK to have copper attached to brass, and most scrap yards allow chrome covering over brass, as well), old aluminum, shiny aluminum (often aluminum heat sinks), and a smaller box for silver and gold contacts and components I intend to break down for precious metal content.

If there are computer hard drives in the pile, they usually require their own special boxes for material that will be sold separately, or they will be sent to Boardsort.

I usually keep another box of copper / aluminum heat sinks, and later take the Dremel to the copper wire. If you use the cut-off disk on the Dremel, you can slice the copper all the way down to the spool, and then peel off the copper. Place the copper in your shiny copper box, and save the heat sink bases. They are often stainless steel, and can be sold separately at scrap yards for decent money. You will find a lot of large heat sinks in old electronics and appliances. I found a heat sink several days ago in a 1950s industrial washing machine that had ten pounds of copper spooled inside it ($30, right there!). The stainless steel base also weighed 18 pounds.

Boardsort also offers a fixed rate for wire and cord connectors that contain gold. Many computer connectors that resemble bristles at the ends, or have many tiny holes contain small amounts of gold and silver. Ribbon ends also frequently contain precious metals. You may decide to save these connectors in a box, and sell them on eBay, as well.

Most scrap dealers buy components containing copper as 'Copper Breakage' or 'Electric Motors'. Save components containing copper in a box. Many of these components can also be easily broken open with a hammer or cut open with a Dremel, and then you can remove the copper and brass pieces that are inside to maximize your profits.

Make sure that you are keeping an eye out for precious metal contacts while you are scrapping. Old electronics and appliances can have relatively large contacts that are often almost pure silver, and sometimes gold. Look on the ends of brass and copper fingers where wires are connected, inside all electric motors, and inside any components that spin at high speeds or generate a lot of heat.

Contacts can range in size from the width of a pencil lead all the way up to the diameter of a large watch battery. Many gold contacts will be bright and shiny gold-colored buttons. They are easy to spot, as gold does not tarnish. Silver contacts can be more difficult to find, as they are often dulled and tarnished with age, and can blend in with the base material.

If you are unsure if the contacts are silver or gold, lightly scrape them with a screwdriver, or hit them with the Dremel disk. They will be bright and shiny under the exterior coating of grime. If you're still not sure, test with your gold tester, or throw them in your 'Gold and Silver' box and refine it with the rest of the material in the box later.

When you find good contacts, clip the button of silver or gold off, and then keep the base material for brass or copper scrap. Don't waste the whole brass or copper finger by refining it in your gold and silver material.

When you fill up the Flat Rate boxes, photograph the materials inside, weigh the box (take a photo of the box with the scale read-out), label the box with the weight, and then list the material on eBay, or save it to take to the scrap dealer.

The last step is the most important. Make sure that you clean up your mess after you are done bashing electronics! If you do your business inside, your significant other will not be happy with the end result of your destruction. If they are not happy, then you will not be happy either, right? Happy wife, happy life!

If you have an outdoor shop or disassembly area, you should still clean up the mess. Metal pieces can be sharp, and kids or pets can get cut on them.

HOW TO SELL YOUR GOLD AND SILVER FOR MAXIMUM PROFIT

There are many investors looking to take advantage of the security of investing in gold and silver. The risk is considerably less than speculating on the stock market. Gold and silver are commodities with a finite supply. It is getting harder and harder to find, so the spot price is going to continue to trend upward over time for both metals.

The question for many gold and silver scrappers is: Do I save the scrap gold and silver and cash in several years after the gold prices advance, or do I cash in my gold immediately?

As we talked about earlier, I have been saving my gold for several years now. I think that it's going to be a nice little kitty in several years, when our family is going to be paying for college tuitions.

However, you may opt to cash in your gold, silver and platinum as you collect it. This can be accomplished in several different ways.

Before you sell your treasure, you MUST know its current value. This is vital. Regardless of which method you use to sell your gold and silver, you have to make sure that you know how much it is worth so you don't get ripped off.

These are the steps I use to sell large lots of precious metals:

1) Separate the lot into potential collectibles and those scrap metals that you will be selling purely for scrap value. Further divide the scrap precious metals by type of metal and purity, so that you have piles of scrap silver and silver contacts, sterling silver, scrap gold and gold contacts, 14K marked gold, 10K marked gold, gold-filled, etc. Keep each additional metal separate (platinum, etc.).

2) Use your jewelry scale and weigh each pile in grams. After you weigh each pile, put the contents into a container and mark the outside of the container with its contents and the weight in grams.

3) Start a ledger page and record each container and the weight.

4) Use the precious metals calculators to determine value by spot price, as explained earlier in this book. Record the values of each container on the ledger and record the spot price that you used to determine the value. Remember, the spot price is constantly changing, so when you actually get your metals assayed, the spot price will be a bit higher or lower than when you figured the value for yourself.

If you take your precious metals to a local assayer or jeweler to get an assayed value or quote, take the ledger with you. Record any offers that you receive on your ledger, so that you can compare them later. Never accept the first offer that you receive, unless you have been doing business with that person or business for a while and trust them.

If somebody is offering you a great price, it is only because the demand is very high. Check at other locations. You may get an even higher offer.

Selling Precious Metals to a Refiner

When you are selling to a large refinery, you are selling precious metals to a company that specializes in the buying and selling of metals. You have the security of knowing who you are selling your valuable metals to, as long as you select an established refinery.

The process is fairly straightforward and each website spells out their PM buying process for you, so it is easy to sell your metals. Some companies will even send you an empty container for your gold, with a return address on it. You put your gold in the container and your information on the enclosed form and then drop it in the mail. The company's address and postage is already on the box.

When the company gets your package, they assay your metals and make you an offer based on current spot prices. Typically, you can expect to get 90-95% of the current spot price offered to you.

You have several days to consider their offer. If you accept, they pay you via check or using an online payment service such as Paypal. If you decline the offer, they ship your metal back to you.

The process is similar at physical refineries. They assay your gold or silver, and issue you a check for the value on site if you accept the offer.

If you decide to go this route, I would recommend getting several assays before you accept an offer. There can be a wide range of offers from different refineries. I have seen articles online that say that gold buyers have sent the same package to several refineries and had offers vary by up to $150 on $1500 worth of gold!

One other thing to consider is that some refineries require minimum amounts of metals before they will accept a package from customers. There are some companies that will accept smaller amounts, but they pay out at lower percentages of current spot prices.

Here are a couple of refineries to consider (I do not make any recommendation on which refinery to use, and receive nothing for providing these links. They are just a starting point for your research.)

http://www.midwestrefineries.com/ - Large refinery that is often preferred by forum members on TreasureNet.com and ScrapMetalJunkie.com. Pay 95% for gold, 90% for sterling. No minimum amount of material is required, no fees.

http://www.apmr.com/ - Large refinery that buys most precious metals. Charges 10% + $25 assay fee, which is acceptable. Does not charge more fees for smaller lots.

http://www.dillongage.com/ - Offers 98% for less than 49oz of gold, 99% over. $150 fee. Have option of receiving payment in gold bars.

http://preciousmetalsreclaiming.com/ - Buys scrap gold and silver and contacts

http://directgold.metallixrefining.com/ - Buys small lots of gold, platinum, silver. Rates are a bit lower, but good source for selling small lots of metals.

Selling Precious Metals On EBay

I have a lot of experience selling items on eBay, including precious metals. There are advantages and disadvantages to selling your gold and silver there.

ADVANTAGES:

- Quickest turnaround – Unless you selling to a physical refinery near you, eBay is the fastest way to sell. You can even set your auction to 1-day to take advantage of a spot price spike.
- The best online location to sell collectible precious metal items like vintage jewelry and sterling silver decorative items. Bidders of collectible items will sometimes surpass the precious metal value due to the collectible value on antiques.
- Potential for items to be sold for premium prices. You never know when bidders will compete for your lot and send it higher than you thought that you could make for the lot.

- It's fun. You get to watch your auction and see how high the bid price goes. In the last couple of minutes, you may get to watch your auction price shoot up, as "eBay snipers" try to scoop it up at the last second.

DISADVANTAGES:

- You have to deal with eBay's crappy customer service department and their payment service Paypal. Many sellers have had negative issues with Paypal refunding payments from buyers who file false claims. eBay almost always sides with the buyer, not the seller (you) in any issues involving complaints.
- You have to pay eBay fees and Paypal fees.
- If bidders don't bid, you can potentially have auctions end significantly under the spot price. This is usually not the case, as the number of gold and silver buyers on eBay routinely keeps ending auction prices close to current spot prices.
- You have to photograph your lot, make a listing, securely package your items and ship them. For experienced eBay sellers, this is not an issue. If you are new to selling on eBay, the process is not difficult, but there is a learning curve involved and it takes time to list your items.

For me, I have sold collectible items on eBay for years, so it was an easy transition to selling metals there. Just make sure that if you sell high value precious metal items, you cover your butt. Take multiple photos of the items for the eBay auction, so bidders can plainly see any defects. Write good descriptions and do not exaggerate to make your item sound better than it is. Provide the exact weight of the item in grams or troy ounces.

Make sure that that bidder knows what they are going to be getting if they win the auction.

After the auction is over and you have accepted payment through Paypal, securely package your item in a sturdy box. I would recommend that you charge enough for shipping so that you can include USPS insurance for items over $100.

Refining Your Own Precious Metals

The third avenue for your consideration is more risky, but also will yield the highest value for your scrap precious metals. If you can effectively refine your own metal, you cut out several "middle-men", and get the most value from your hard work. This method may also be the only way to harvest actual precious metal value from plated gold and silver, as I have yet to find a refiner that will accept plated material, due to the cost associated with separating the precious metal from the base metal.

You must consider that the refining of precious metals is a risky business for beginners. The refining processes require the use of caustic materials, including very strong acids. They also take some time and effort, and you will have to purchase chemicals and hardware to complete the refining. Many of the people that refine their own metals enjoy the process of refining and have a background in chemistry or laboratory work.

If you choose to take this route, **you do so at your own risk**. Refining precious metals can emit noxious vapors and the acids can cause severe burns. You must have a secure area in which to refine, where you have a ventilation system and you can keep children away from. This is not a suggestion. It is necessity!

There are many different methods for refining precious metals, and I have not tried any of them, opting instead to hoard my gold and silver, with the eventual goal of selling to a reputable precious metal buyer. I do not recommend any one method of refining. It is up to you to decide after completing your research.

There are many different methods for refining precious metals, which can be found online through your research.

Web pages for refining gold and silver:

http://www.ehow.com/how_7830442_refine-gold-plating.html

https://www.ishor.com/RefineAgInstruct.php

TAKING YOUR PRECIOUS METALS BUSINESS TO THE NEXT LEVEL: HOW TO GUARANTEE CONSISTENT SOURCES OF METAL

After you have been buying and selling precious metals for a while and have gotten proficient, the next step is to establish yourself as a legitimate business in your community.

The thought of actually "owning a business" is intimidating to some people, especially those that have been trying to make ends meet for a while. But, there really is not much that you have to do differently.

You do not have to have a separate physical building for your business. You can work out of your home. You don't need a business license in most places for this type of home business, although you should check with your governing municipality. That way, you will know when you need to become licensed, so that you can avoid legal problems.

In order to establish yourself as a legitimate precious metals buyer, you really only have to do several things:

1. Promote a professional image.
2. Relay contact information and communicate to PM sellers in several formats
3. Have enough funding so that you can pay for metals on a schedule

4. Be prepared to advertise your business

This sounds harder than it really is. Let's take a look at each step in more detail.

Professional Image

This is the easiest one. Just make sure that you look like a person that is trustworthy and that businesses would want to deal with.

Dress in what I would deem 'semi-professional' attire. You don't have to look like you're dressed for prom. Wear something respectable, like khakis and a collared shirt. Some people wear jeans, but why not wear something a little nicer? A tie doesn't hurt, either. Whatever you do, don't wear shorts, or a baseball cap.

If at all possible, drive a decent looking vehicle. You will be parking in front of businesses. You don't want to be pulling to the door up in a vehicle with no muffler. You don't want your truck to shake violently and then backfire when you get out of the vehicle to walk in. Chick…Chick…Chick…Boom! [Everybody instinctively ducks]

Communication and Contact Information

This entails being able to give business managers or owners a way to get a hold of you when they have materials or questions for you. This is also simple to accomplish.

You can start out by having some business cards printed up for you. Websites like VistaPrint will print 250 business cards for about $10, with free shipping. Don't try to make yourself free business cards in order to save a buck. You want a business card that you are confident handing to people.

To start out, you really only have to have your name and what you buy as the title line on the business card. Something like: 'ERIC MICHAEL, BUYER OF PRECIOUS METALS AND SCRAP GOLD' will work. OF course, if you can come up with a catchy business name and a logo, that looks even more professional.

Make sure that you have your name, your telephone numbers (especially your cell phone number) and your social media URL(s) on the card.

I would highly recommend that you set up a Facebook business page and Twitter account for your business. These pages are free on both sites and they increase your professional image. It is also sometimes more convenient for businesses to send you a tweet or Facebook message than it is for them take the time to call you. Anything that you can do to make things easier for people increases the probability that you will land agreements with businesses.

Facebook and Twitter are also excellent networking opportunities. You will meet other buyers and sellers in your area of expertise Businesses will be able to find *you*, instead of you having to hunt *them* down all of the time.

Manta.com is another free online networking opportunity worth registering on. Manta is a directory of local businesses that allows owners to network with each other. It could also be another way for precious metal sellers to make contact with you. Setting up a business page on Manta is very easy and it costs nothing, so why not use it?

Funding

This only requires that you have enough money to pay businesses on a regular basis when you buy metals. Remember, these contacts will be continually generating scrap metal for you to buy. You have to be able to pay them on site, or you will lose the contact.

Make sure that you settle on the methods of payment when you set up the contact. Most established businesses will accept credit cards. This makes things very easy. You may wish to eventually get a business credit card to keep accounts separate, but to start out, it is not necessary.

Some businesses will require cash, or perhaps they accept checks. Make sure when you set up the agreement for you to purchase metal that you know how the account manager wants to be paid and how often they want you to buy metals.

Advertising

There are many sources of free advertising that will help you to get your business off of the ground. You can post an ad for free in many locations, including Craigslist, Facebook groups, Twitter and eBay Announcements.

You can also post physical flyers or posters in advantageous locations, where many people will see them, like malls, store entryways and colleges. It will cost you a couple dollars to have the flyers printed, but if you even get one contact that ends up being a lead, you have paid for all of your advertising costs for months!

Another very effective way to advertise is to put your business information on your vehicle. VistaPrint offers car door magnets and window decals starting at only $12. Think about how many people see your car when you are driving on the expressway on a busy day. It also looks impressive when you pull up to a business to buy metals and you have your cool logo on your vehicle.

You can start out with free advertising, but it is a mistake to not advertise at all. Start out small and work your way up from there. But, understand this. It is very important to advertise, if you want your business to be successful.

Now that we have established what we need to do to be able to professionally manage our business, let's talk about what types of accounts we are going to be attempting to set up.

What we will be aiming for is businesses that generate a constant flow of metals that we can immediately sell for profit. Once you start thinking about places that generate scrap precious metals, you will come up with more and more places to go to set up accounts.

You will be amazed how quickly your business can grow by establishing even a couple regular metal pick-ups with the right businesses. It is easy to take your business from a part-time paycheck to a regular source of income for family.

The hardest thing for most people to do is to go into the first business and talk to somebody. JUST DO IT, BABY! You owe it to yourself and your family to give yourself the opportunity to succeed.

Think of it this way. You are going to significantly help out the manager of the businesses that you are trying to establish an agreement with. Sometimes, you will be offering them money for stuff that they didn't even know was valuable! Other times, businesses will have established agreements with other metals buyers, and you will be offering them considerably more than they get paid from the other guys or gals.

EXPECT TO HEAR 'NO'! You can actually practice this, and it is a good laugh, but it helps to set you up for success. Get your buddy or spouse to listen to your pitch and act like a business manager. Tell them to keep saying 'no' to you in different ways. No, no, no. It is actually a funny little exercise, but it gets you ready to talk to people. Give your best pitch and be confident, but expect managers to say 'no', especially at first.

Do not accept 'no' as a final answer. It can often be a person's initial reaction to say no to somebody that they have not dealt with. Continue on with your conversation. Keep it non-confrontational and friendly. "I can respect that you have had a deal with the pawn shop for a while, but can I ask you what percentage of spot price they pay you for your material? What? They won't give you a specific percentage? I'm not surprised. I'll tell you what... I'll weigh your material in your shop here and cut you a check based on 60% of spot price every two weeks. I can pretty much guarantee you that the pawn shop is not paying you anywhere near that much."

You want to land agreements with businesses, especially for the first couple of months. Be willing to pay more than what you would prefer to pay to establish the agreement. Remember, you know exactly how much the material is worth after doing your calculations. You can turn around and make a profit, even if you have to buy at 80-85% of spot price to top another buyer.

Once you have established communication with a business, MAINTAIN IT. Do everything that you can do to become friends with the manager or owner. Make it very hard for them to want to do business with anybody else. Bring them in doughnuts when you come. Make them up a 'plaque of appreciation' that they can hang in their store... whatever it takes.

BUSINESSES THAT GENERATE SCRAP PRECIOUS METALS

There are long lists of the types of businesses that you should be contacting to establish arrangements to buy precious metals from, but I will mention of few of them to get you thinking about where to start:

Thrift Stores, Antique Shops and Second-Hand Stores

These stores will not generate a ton of precious metals for you, but you can often get them for extremely cheap. You can even contact the owner or manager of places that have stuff donated to them and ask them if they would be willing to give you first offer on donated sterling silver and marked gold. This can yield some great prices!

Another route that you can take with donated precious metals is to have an arrangement set up to buy the sterling and marked gold at a specific rate. Some second-hand stores will already have made deals with local pawn shops or PM buyers to buy their stuff, but the rates are usually low – 30-40% of spot. If you can offer an extra 10% of spot price, you can easily snag the store away from the other buyer.

These stores are also a source of FREE precious metals. You can ask if you can drop off a box and have the employees put their broken jewelry and sterling silver decorative items in it. They can't put them on the floor to sell, so they will occasionally just give you the items! This is also a great way to get PM-bearing vintage electronics and collectibles. Ask if you can haul away their unsold items and broken electronics once every couple weeks, or whenever they contact you and let you know the box is full.

These are often the easiest businesses in which to get your foot in the door. Many of them don't have any buyers for PMs and the ones that do have been getting ripped off for years!

Lost and Founds

Businesses that have lost-and-founds are an outstanding source of low-cost PMs. Many businesses do not have any policies about what they do with unclaimed items, so what happens to those items? Most expensive gold items will get claimed by employees of the business, but you would be surprised how often these items just get tossed in the boxes and forgotten about.

If you make arrangements to empty out their bins or pay them for the valuable contents, you will get 90% of the good stuff. Once your agreement is in place, most companies will specify that employees cannot remove items from lost-and-found bins without consequences, since you are paying the company for their contents.

This is also another great source of items that can be sold on eBay or Amazon for "bonus money".

Which types of places have good lost-and-founds? Think big. Hospitals, department stores, malls, college buildings, governmental offices, stadiums and office buildings all have large lost-and-founds.

Dentists, Doctors and Hospitals

What do these places have that we would be looking for....? How about almost high-yielding gold and silver? Most dentists keep a supply of scrap gold that was generated when they made fillings, crowns and other pieces, or from when they replaced people's existing dental work. Dentists' offices will also generate gold-bearing sludge from when they make their gold fillings. Most dentists know that their scrap gold is valuable and have arrangements set up with PM buyers to pay them for it.

However, there is not a lot of competition for these accounts. Many dentists have to ship their scrap to get paid for it, or they may have a company that only picks up their scrap a couple of times a year.

If you can offer a more competitive deal and agree to pay them more often and pay them for all of their different types of scrap PMs, you can often snag these valuable accounts. You may even find that old dentist that has been hoarding his gold for twenty years and just has not had the right deal come along yet!

Similar deals can be made with medical professionals that use X-ray machines, as they generate silver-bearing X-ray negatives and the slurry used to develop the X-rays also contains silver. Think about locations where large amounts of X-rays are stored. Hospitals will usually have an account set up for selling the silver, but again, they often only receive 30-40% of the actual silver value from their buyers. Professional photography studios also generate silver-bearing material during photograph processing and in their negatives.

Jewelers and Jewelry Repair Shops

There is going to be competition for the scrap PMs generated by jewelry stores and repair shops, but these can be sources of a LOT of gold. They are worth your time to pursue, even if it takes a couple of times to swing a deal. Owners and managers of these businesses always know what the spot prices of PMs are and the value of their "sweeps" and gold dust generated during the manufacture and repair processes.

But, the scraps have to be bought by somebody and it might as well be you. Just be prepared to pay close to spot price for the value of the scrap.

Gold and Silver Manufacturing Shops

Think about businesses near you that may use gold or other PMs when they are making items that they sell. What do they do with their scrap gold? Obviously, if they are making items out of gold, they know about its value. However, most will have buyers for their scrap, so you just have to work your magic to start buying their gold.

Gold and silver plating companies, trophy makers, clock makers and repair and any other companies that use gold plating on the exterior of their items are good places to start.

Auto Shops, Scrap Yards and Car Dealerships

What does an auto shop have that I want, you might ask? If you are already a scrapper, you know the answer to that question. Platinum.

All vehicles manufactured for the United States after 1975 were required to have catalytic converters in the exhaust systems for emission control. These "cats", as they are known to scrappers, contain platinum pellets inside of them. Cats can worth as much as $150 a piece!

You will want to educate yourself on cats and the values of particular styles of converters. Here is a start:

Most of the shops and dealers understand the PM value of cats. They will have them saved in a large box in the shop, in most cases. Most shops will have buyers for their converters, but these buyers are often unreliable and unprofessional. If you show up in nice clothes and explain what you are willing to pay and agree to show up when they ask and pay them immediately, you can often garner a deal with these businesses.

One source of platinum that a fair amount of shops and businesses do NOT know about, on the other hand, is that oxygen sensors (or O2 sensors) also contain a small amount of platinum.

Oxygen sensors generally only contain about $1 worth of platinum each, but most shops will throw them in a box for you, often for no cost. Many places do not even know that they hold value. Auto shops will collect quite a few oxygen sensors in a short amount of time, so it can be another consistent source of easy money for you.

Cell Phone, Computer and Electronics Repair Shops

All cell phones contain gold inside of the devices. Many of them can also be sold online to websites that specialize in buying and repairing old cell phones. Even old, outdated cell phones have value. If you can negotiate a deal with cell phone repair or sales businesses, you can set up a constant supply of "Almost Free Gold".

Computer shops and electronics repair shops are a great source of free PMs, as well. Some owners save their PM-bearing scraps and circuit boards, but many don't. Many of these businesses will let you haul away their scraps and dead computers for free. It saves them having to dispose of them.

Just be prepared to do some disassembly to process this material and you will need some room to work, as this stuff is big and bulky. Even so, if you are not a scrapper-at-heart and don't like working with your hands, you can still either sell the computers whole to scrap yards as E-waste or quickly strip the CPU and gold bearing circuit boards in several minutes.

We will talk more about how to process electronics and computers for PMs later in this book.

ARE GOLD PLATED AND SILVER PLATED ITEMS WORTH BUYING?

As we discussed earlier in this book, the thickness of the plating on decorative items and jewelry can vary greatly, depending on when it was made. Since the price of gold skyrocketed to up over $500 in 1980, manufacturers have become much more careful with how much gold is applied when plating items.

Since the 1980s, most gold plated items have a minute amount of gold covering the base metal. This gold plating is of such a small amount, that it makes stripping the gold plating from the base metal for its gold value a futile exercise – a total waste of time.

Silver plated items are also tough to make money from, as far as the precious metal value. The spot price of silver does not allow a scrapper to recover enough material to make the stripping of the plating cost-effective, unless it is very think plating, as we referred to earlier.

Stripping gold and silver yourself is very dangerous. People have died attempting to process their own gold. I do not recommend that anybody attempt to reclaim plated gold without a chemistry or laboratory background. This is no place for a hobbyist.

Now… having said that, and I'm not speaking to the veracity of this report… I read a book by a woman who said that she regularly made $600 a week by locating gold plated items at thrift stores, along with the random sterling silver and karat gold items that she came across. This was in the 1990s, when gold was only $400 an ounce.

If what she said were true, she would be making a lot more than that now, with the increase in the current price of gold. The way that she said that she made most of her money was by finding the thickly plated gold items manufactured in the 1960s and 70s, when gold was still only $50 an ounce. She had a process for stripping the gold off of the base materials over the course of two weeks and she ended up with 99.9% gold pellets.

Again, I'm not saying that there is any value in plated gold. Most people say that it is worthless, except for the collectible value of vintage pieces. I'm telling you that there are people that say that some plated items contain a fair amount of gold and can be processed (I can't stress this enough – leave the gold processing to the professionals).

I mention this mainly because I have been saving gold plated items from the 1960s and 1970s. There were some big heavy pieces that were totally covered with thickly plated gold from that time period – big heavy lamps, light stands, flower pot holders, etc. There is the potential to reclaim some gold from these items.

I found almost all of these items for free at yard sales and in junk piles. You will also see them in thrift stores for $1-2, so I have bought them when I find them at those prices. I have not processed any of them yet to see what they yield. I have thought about attempting to scrape the outer layer off with an abrasive and some elbow grease to see what I get.

Either way, you will come out ahead with these large items, if you are a scrapper. The scrap metal value of the base metal will cover the small price that you paid for the items. The electric items also contain copper wiring which can be sold for scrap and the vintage components, knobs and handles can be sold on eBay for good money.

Another thing worth noting is that many gold and silver plated items cover semi-valuable metals like copper and brass. Scrap copper can be sold at a scrap yard for about $3/LB and scrap brass goes for about $2, so these big heavy plated items can make you some easy money.

Vintage silver-plate items can also be very collectible and sold to antique stores or on eBay for much more than the cost of the items at thrift stores. Individual silver-plate serving pieces and table ware can be sold for excellent money on eBay or on Replacements.com.

So, although you will read online and hear from other sellers that plated items are crap, there is money to be made if you know how to sell it. Is it as profitable as sterling silver or karat gold? Of course not, but if you find it for free, you should understand that it has value in some circumstances.

A SECRET 'NON-PRECIOUS METAL' MORE VALUABLE THAN SILVER?

What if I told you that lead was more valuable than silver? You would laugh at me, right? We'll see who laughs last.

Generally the scrap metal value of lead is only about 50 cents a pound, which does not seem like much, although even a small piece of lead can yield $10 due to its weight. The lead content of car batteries is the reason why they are worth $5-8 each.

That's for everyday lead. There is another type of lead that is much more valuable.

It's called low-alpha lead (LAL). When lead comes out of the earth and is refined for use in manufacturing, it is slightly radioactive. As lead ages, it loses that radioactivity. After 22 years, lead is basically inert. This antique lead is known as low-alpha lead.

After lead is not radioactive, it becomes safe to handle and is valuable for use in scientific experimentation, large semiconductors, high-value electronics solder and high level computer applications.

Most of the buyers looking for LAL seem to prefer lead that is very old, even prior to the 1700s, however it seems that any LAL that has been in the ground or underwater since before World

War 2 (1945) can be used as LAL, and is valuable. This is due to the decay rates in the element lead (and perhaps partially due to atmospheric radiation levels since 1945).

Either way, some very wealthy companies need LAL for high tech applications. The exact value of LAL is not known, but there have been claims online of people being paid up to $300/LB for high-end LAL from old shipwrecks.

Very few people know about the value of LAL and even fewer know where to sell it. There are no buyers of LAL that advertise online that I was able to locate, but there are people that say that they have sold it for over $180/LB.

I've been saving my vintage lead that I've found with my metal detector for a while. Maybe this will have a market in the mainstream soon, as more applications for its use develop. If so, I will be glad that I saved old lead for several years. Perhaps you will, too! Or, maybe you will take the extra initiative to find out who is buying this stuff right now. I'm sure that it would be well worth your time, if you have access to a supply of LAL.

For more information on low-alpha lead, check out www.scrapmetaljunkie.com/68/how-to-sell-scrap-**lead**

Here is another interesting debate on LAL value: http://www.treasurenet.com/forums/shipwrecks/105653-low-alpha-antiquity-lead.html

THANK YOU, READERS!

Thank you for taking the time to read this book. I hope that you enjoyed it as much as I enjoyed researching the background content and putting this book together.

Please put your mind to immediately applying what you learned here in Almost Free Gold. DO NOT wait until next week or next month to start! You can find items to sell in any location, and at any time of the year.

This information is best used in concert with the rest of the Almost Free Money books. While you are looking for gold and silver, you *will* have the opportunity to buy many other valuable sources of profit for you and your family. The key is to recognize these items when you see them, especially when they are free or very cheap. Continue to research and diversify other items that will contribute to the success of your business.

YOU have to make up your mind to get the ball rolling, and it will be all downhill from there. I hope that you will have as much fun as my family and I have finding treasure for free, or plucking dusty gems from garage sales and thrift stores.

If you have any questions, contact me on my Facebook page, on Twitter, or email me at almostfreemoney@yahoo.com. I would like to hear from you!

If you feel that this book has helped you to find new and enjoyable ways to make money or save your family's cash, I humbly ask you for only two things. #1, tell your family and friends about this book, and #2, please take several seconds to leave positive feedback regarding this book on its Amazon Detail Page. Positive feedback directly affects other readers' reviews and leads to additional orders, and the proceeds from this book will go directly into my sons' college funds.

I also have a new offer for Almost Free Money series fans (and it's a fun project). Record a short video discussing the benefits that you received from reading Almost Free Money books. It does not have to be long. The video will be used on the Eric Michael Books blog and on YouTube to help promote the books. In exchange, I will provide you with a hyperlink so that you can share it with your friends and family. If you are an author or have your own website of Facebook fan page, I will link the video to your webpage. And, I will give you FREE PDF copies of any Almost Free Money books that you do not already have, and will send you FREE copies of any future titles before they are available to the public. That's a sweet deal! Just send your video to me at almostfreemoney@yahoo.com.

WEBSITES AND LINKS

Here are some very helpful websites and web pages to jump start your research. These are my favorites, after many hours of surfing (You are welcome!)

1. http://www.scrapmetaljunkie.com/scrap-metal-handbook-guide

I still can't believe this site is free. A tremendous amount of information, and well organized. The site provides a nice explanation on how to sort and identify scrap metals.

This is the only site that I have found that provides step-by-step instructions on how to disassemble appliances and other large items for maximizing scrap recovery.

The website has pages on how to take apart a TV, computer, washing machine, microwave, and many other electronics and appliances, in order to harvest precious metals and scrap metals.

It also has an excellent blog, with information from many experienced scrappers. Regardless of whether you are a beginner, or an experienced scrapper, if you have not been to this site, you will make money by spending time here.

2. http://www.scribd.com/doc/20327561/Scrap-Parts-Comp-Identification#outer_page_1

Scraper's Master Parts List: A nice summation of where you can find valuable gold, silver and platinum in computers and other electronics. Indexed, with photo identification of components like diodes, transformers, and capacitors and where to find them within the electronics. It even gives you a photo of each component and tells you what PMs are contained within the components.

If you are into harvesting free PMs, this is location to start and spend some time. The photos are excellent, which is why I did not provide photos in this book.

3. http://boardsort.com

This company will pay you up front through PayPal immediately upon confirmation of your information with digital photo of your material. They pay competitive prices for computer scrap, gold board fingers, and some other related e-scrap. You have to pay for shipping, but they pay up front, which is nice. They also have an updated price list of what they pay for a variety of materials, so you know what you can expect to be paid when you send them your scrap.

4. http://www.replacements.com/misc/selltous.htm

Replacements.com is an excellent place to sell silverware, sterling silver tableware and collectibles, china and other collectible pieces. Also has photos of hundreds of different patterns of silverware and collectibles to identify what you have. To sell, you fill out a form, they make you an offer and then you ship your pieces to them.

5. http://www.treasurenet.com/forums/garage-sale-finds/

A great forum for treasure hunters of multiple persuasions. You can learn a ton here and it's easy to get hooked on other types of treasure hunting. If you want to talk to treasure hunting experts, this is the place.

6. http://www.scrapmetalforum.com/

A very active scrap metal forum and a great place to learn about finding scrap PMs and how to process and sell them. There is an excellent resource for locating buyers of many vintage electronics scrap that you won't find anywhere else, including buyers for tantalum capacitors, high value carbide steel, etc. http://www.scrapmetalforum.com/scrap-buyers-sellers/

7. http://www.ehow.com/how_7830442_refine-gold-plating.html

How to refine your scrap and plated gold to .995 pure. Requires chemicals and safety equipment. Do this at your own risk.

8. http://www.globemetal.com/recycling/?bm_uri=recycling/tantalum-scrap/

Buyers of tantalum scrap found in electronics / capacitors.

9. http://cointrackers.com/is-my-coin-silver.php

Good information on silver coins, and actual silver content. Did you know that a 1963 US quarter is worth $3.98 due to silver content?!

10. http://www.metalprices.com

Spot prices for most precious and scrap metals, plus historical prices, with graphs.

11. http://iscrapapp.blogspot.com/

Another good source of scrap metal information and an active forum

RECOMMENDED PAY SITES:

How to Make Money in the Home-Based Salvage and Recycling Business

The Author does an excellent job giving step by step instructions for starting your own business or second income by recycling scrap metal and electronics. Personal stories about how the author got started and took his business to the next level.

He provides many examples of materials that you can make good money on that you can find anywhere. Includes salvage of gold and silver from electronics. Well-organized and easy to read. Also affordable, as well. Worth the cost of the document.

The Complete Battery Reconditioning Report

This document pays for itself, as soon as you recondition your first battery instead of buying a new one. I use this information all the time. Very easy to use information on how to recharge supposedly dead NiCad, NiMH and Lead Acid batteries. Most of the techniques can be applied for free, and the author gives you an excellent and unique way to start a new or second income in any locale. Highly recommended.

How to Make Money Buying and Selling Gold: A Gold Buying System

Includes premade flyers and advertisements for your business and instruction for starting a gold buying business, where you buy from residents in your town for excellent profits. Everything you need to start buying scrap gold and jewelry and become the go-to person in your community with low start-up costs.

SOURCES

Andrews, Scott. *High-Profit Recycling: Insider's Secrets of a Recycling Entrepreneur*. 2006

Connor, David H. *Your Neighborhood Gold Mine*. David H. Connor. 2013

Moore, Megan. *Thrift Store Prospecting: How to Find Gold and Silver for Recovery in Thrift Stores*. Penultimate Vision. 1990

Priebe, Vicki. *Cheap Gold and Silver: How to Find Amazing Deals on Gold and Silver*. iFind Entertainment. 2012

ADDITIONAL RESEARCH

Since the initial release of Almost Free Money, the series has experienced rapid growth. The series now contains six volumes. Three of the books have become #1 Amazon Kindle bestsellers.

Our Almost Free Money Nation mailing list features instant notification of new book releases and free advance reading chapters. It also provides free giveaways and provides information on the hottest blog posts, without sending any spam or advertising to your inbox.

Eric Michael has developed two websites that offer free information on a wide variety of subjects that can broaden your internet selling portfolio:

http://www.ericmichaelbooks.com is more than just the home of the Almost Free Money series. It is also a fully-functioning blog with over 60 pages of information on selling on Amazon, eBay and Etsy, flipping used items for profit, selling scrap metal, locating precious metals and selling free items on the internet.

http://www.garagesaleacademy.com is another busy hub for garage sale, yard sale and flea market hosts, shoppers and flippers. The site offers many valuable tips on organizing, advertising and pricing at sales and flea markets for maximum profit. GSA also hosts a very popular page for the World's Longest Garage Sale and allows garage sale shoppers to discuss their finds and advice.

All of the Almost Free Money books (both Kindle and softcover book editions) can be found at the Eric Michael Amazon Author Page.

While you are there, please stop in and say hi at the bottom of the page, link to my social media pages and a 'Like' in the top corner would be much appreciated!

Here is a very brief summary of several of the Almost Free Money books:

1) Passive Income for Life (#1 Kindle bestseller, top ten for 8 months straight): How to develop a home internet business that provides passive income paychecks for as long as you maintain your business. Make money while you sleep by building an Amazon business selling used items that you can find for under $1 at second hand locations.

2) The Almost Free Money Triple Play Value Pack: Contains the three bestselling AFM books: Almost Free Money, Passive Income for Life and Garage Sale Superstar. A great buy at $5-6!

3) Fast Cash: Selling Used Items for Profit: Learn how to find the best items at second-hand locations and build your own business on Amazon, eBay and Etsy. Contains tips for improving your eBay listings, building your brand, securely shipping items and saving money on overhead.

4) Garage Sale Superstar: Learn how to make the most profit possible at your next garage sale. Tips on organizing, advertising and pricing at garage sales, yard sales and estate sales.

ABOUT THE AUTHOR

Eric Michael is married and is a proud father of two energetic sons. He enjoys family outings and many outdoor activities, including fishing, hunting and camping.

The information provided in the Almost Free Money series was compiled after twelve years of internet research and personal experiences developed a unique skill set – the ability to find a diverse selection of free items (or priced under $1) that could be sold on the internet for surprisingly good money.

In that time period, Mr. Michael has sold well over 10,000 unique items that were located for under $1 on the internet at an average price of over $10 an item. The Almost Free Money system has given his family the second income necessary to allow a parent to stay at home with his two boys, instead of paying for day care.

He has gone on to develop a popular website titled Garage Sale Academy that incorporates portions of Almost Free Money, and expands into other arenas of profiting from flipping garage sale, thrift store and flea market finds, as well as helping garage sale hosts make maximum cash at their sales. He also hosts Facebook fan pages for Almost Free Money and Garage Sale Academy.

www.ingramcontent.com/pod-product-compliance
Lightning Source LLC
Chambersburg PA
CBHW051723170526
45167CB00002B/780